TAROT
The Dark Art

Edward Gordon

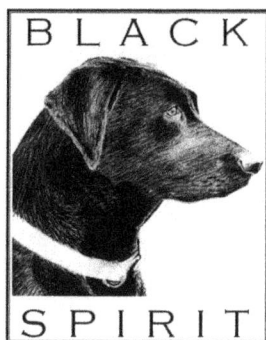

BLACK

SPIRIT

Black Spirit Publishing
P.O. Box 2428, PMB# 8443
Pensacola, FL 32513

ISBN 978-0-9838971-6-3

For rights information, contact Black Spirit Publishing by mail or e-mail:

editor@blackspiritpublishing.com

First Edition

10 9 8 7 6 5 4 3 2 1

For Rebecca,
My Little Scorpio

Table of Contents

QUEEN of SWORDS.

The Queen of Swords: often associated with transformation by way of increased knowledge or wisdom. So, let this be our guiding card!

Introduction

The Sorcery of Tarot

———————— • ————————

There are two ways to approach tarot reading. The first is to do it for entertainment, much like shaking a Magic Eight Ball® and seeing the various responses that pop up in the dark porthole: *Seems unlikely*, *It is decidedly so*, *Try again later*, etc. This is the manner in which most people practice tarot.

It's fun; it's interesting; it's harmless, and there's no need to worry about any negative consequences. It is definitely not dark.

If you go into the French Quarter in New Orleans, which I have done many times, you can get a reading for about $30. There are several new age and Voodoo stores that have readers for the tourists, or you could go into Jackson Square where the readers sit outdoors at card tables and wait for your patronage. It's all good fun. All the readings are bright and positive. All the readings leave you feeling better about yourself. None of them are psychic; none of them are dark.

Then, of course, there is a second way, the original way. It is, quite frankly, the way of the sorcerer and sorceress. It is divination, and it is a form of witchcraft, and when I say witchcraft, I mean *dark* witchcraft.

Now, *dark,* in this context, may not mean what you think it means, and I will cover that more in the last chapter of this book. But for now, realize that if you want serious results from practicing tarot, if you truly want to see the future, if you want the power that comes from being able to provide accurate and insightful readings for yourself and others, then you must treat tarot the way it was always intended to be treated—as sorcery.

By the way, *sorcery*, as a term, has a male and female variation: *Sorcerer* and *Sorceress*. However, the term *sorcerer* actually encapsulates both. It is only the word *sorceress* that creates a distinction. Therefore, in this text, we will use the word *sorcerer* to indicate both male and female practitioners. This will avoid clumsy expressions such as *Sorcerers and sorceresses practice tarot.*

Some people have religious problems with this second way, this *sorcerer's path.* There is an ingrained warning they've learned from childhood. They probably learned it in Sunday school as I did, that sorcery in all its forms is evil.

So long as tarot is just an entertaining card game, there is little violation of religious values, but when it's taken seriously, when it crosses into sorcery, that's when all the warnings of the Bible (if you're a Christian) and the Quran (if you're a Muslim) come to bear.

Quite simply, in those religious systems, sorcerers are to be put to death—no questions, no ambiguity—put to death. And this has been the religious mandate for thousands of years.

Fortunately, in the Western World, no one follows that mandate, but some religious people and churches still consider sorcery to be quite sinful, if not downright Satanic. And many counties and towns still ban fortunetellers from setting up a business or a booth as a result of that religious bias.

But you might ask yourself why the major religions are so opposed to it? The answer, I believe, is that it's a competing and liberating form of individual spiritual power. The form of tarot I will describe in this book produces real results, and that can lead to real spiritual evolution through individual freedom. It necessitates a direct relationship between you and the Divine working in partnership to create the divinatory spell of a tarot reading. It cuts out the middleman of religion. It's hard to see that as a bad thing—but it is certainly a competing thing.

So what path are you willing to take to see the future? What path are you *wanting* to take? I suppose you could use this book for either path. If you want the Magic Eight

Ball® tarot, then study the traditional meanings of the cards, grab a deck and have fun with it. Entertain your family and friends, but if you want more—more is offered.

Practicing tarot as a sorcerer will transform you. It will change the way you think about things and about yourself. It may mean that you are able to leave your spiritual constraints and chains behind you. Certainly, you will come to see things more clearly. You will become a true student of the Divine, and you will learn from the spirit guides the Divine sends to you; not to mention, you will be able to see the future: for yourself and for others.

So, welcome to the dark art of Tarot; let's start our journey!

1

Do You Have Tarot Talent ?

There is a way to determine if your psychic talent includes the practice of tarot divination. There are questions you can ask yourself, and if you answer them, *yes,* then you are suitable to begin your apprenticeship in tarot.

And make no mistake about it; by the time you get to the last page of this book, if you follow the advice and don't rush through it, if you take your time with it, you will emerge a practitioner of the dark art of tarot—and if you are willing, you will emerge as a sorcerer for the Divine.

Granted, if you don't want to take it that far, if you only want to learn tarot enough to have some fun, or create some Halloween entertainment, or dazzle your friends and family at get-togethers, then you need not go all the way through this book. All you need is some cards and the keywords for the cards.

You can get several different kinds of tarot card decks at Amazon.com®, I recommend the Rider-Waite deck. It's the standard. Get it, and then, by all means have fun.

But if you're ready for secrets, if you're ready to delve into symbolism that is thousands of years old, and if you are prepared for that art to change you, to make you darker, stronger, and I believe happier, then you will want to apply your psychic abilities to the tarot. You will want to take the magic into you and ride on the wave of it. It can set you free. What I'm talking about is symbolized by a witch on her broom.

Yes, a flying witch may be a funny image in some contexts, but it's really a symbol of psychic freedom, and thus the freedom of the human soul.

Witches and the Devil flying on brooms. A woodcut from the Malleus Maleficarum, written in 1487. It showed how to detect a witch and examine (torture) her into confessing.

The image on the previous page was taken from the *Malleus Maleficarum* (mal-ee-us mal-ifi-care-um). A book used in the Dark Ages to investigate and prescribe tortures and death to those who used magic of any kind. Sorcery, as a psychic talent, is the soul exercising its freedom in the form of magic. There are still religious forces in this world that would seek to prevent that, but we'll leave that debate for another time.

Let's first find out if you even have a latent psychic ability for tarot.

I will ask you some questions, and you need to answer them honestly to yourself. Think about them, and think if they apply to you at all. If any one of them is true about you, then you can fully apply yourself to learning tarot.

1. Are you attracted to the images you see in the tarot deck?

If you don't have a tarot deck yet, just Google *Tarot Images*. Do you find yourself gazing at them, wondering about them, and in a strange way, attracted to them?

2. Do you have an affinity for symbols?

In other words, do you believe that symbols have power or at least represent forces in the world?

For instance, I don't believe the symbol for Aries in an astrological chart has power in itself. But I do believe it represents a power that exists in our universe, a strange astral power that is all about confidence, power, action, drive, authority, command, and vitality. Taken altogether, I believe there is a force like that which can shape things in the world. In astrology, the force is called *Aries*. Below is the symbol for Aries.

ϒ

Aries

Some people believe quite strongly in symbols and even wear various symbolic talismans on a ring or a necklace. Consider those who wear a St. Christopher's medal, a cross or crucifix, a peace sign, or people who have various symbols as tattoos. Perhaps you are one of these people.

3. Are you interested in what your dreams mean?

Some people couldn't care less about their dreams, other people have a dream, and they see something strange in it, and they wonder what it means. If you are the type of person who wonders about the images they see in their dreams, then you are someone who considers symbols to have messages, and that's a tarot attitude. A tarot attitude only comes from a latent psychic ability for tarot.

4. Do you believe astrological signs represent people?

You might say you know someone who is very Virgo, or a true Capricorn, or you might know your own astrological sun sign and believe it represents you, "I'm a Cancer," or "I'm a Sagittarius." Astrology and tarot are close cousins, so a love of astrology indicates an affinity for tarot.

Have you ever, in your life, experienced precognition?

This could be a dream that came true. It could be a sense that the phone was going to ring and it did, or that someone was on the other end of the phone when it rang, and they were. It could be a premonition or feeling that something bad was about to happen, and then it did—that sort of thing.

Finally, are you currently engaged in any one or all of the following activities:

Mediumship, witchcraft, fortunetelling, tarot reading, palmistry, astrology, direct psychic readings or picture readings, energy healing, angelology, demonology, necromancy, dream interpretation, or crystal gazing?

If you have answered *yes* to any one or more of the above, then you are psychically capable of learning tarot. And because tarot cards are a psychic crutch, very little psychic ability is actually required to produce a good reading. That is to say, tarot reading is not like mediumship or direct psychic readings. Once you learn the cards and apply the appropriate ritual, it's pretty easy to see the psychic story in the cards that produce the reading.

That's what's great about tarot: with it, you can turn on your powers of divination at will. You don't have to wait for inspiration or any particular mood. The Divine magic brings you the right cards, and the pictures trigger your psychic insight. It's fantastically simple!

So, what if you have none of what I've mentioned above? Well, to be quite honest then, I'm surprised you're even interested in tarot, except perhaps as a means of entertainment.

And if you only want to do it for entertainment, again, all you need is a deck of tarot cards and to learn the keywords. The spreads you lay and the predictions you make, just like a Magic Eight Ball®, won't have any real meaning to them, but there's no harm done and nothing to lose.

However, if you have seen, by the previous questions, that you have a latent talent for tarot, don't second guess yourself. Just have that faith in yourself that you can do it, because you can. Don't worry about whether you come from a long line of psychics or that your grandmother wasn't a Wiccan high priestess. None of that matters. If you answered *yes* to any of the previous questions, you have the talent you need for tarot.

So, with that said, let us move forward...

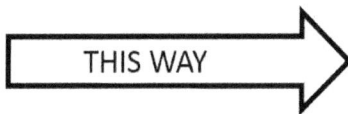

THIS WAY

2

Description and History of the Tarot Deck

Description of the Tarot Deck

Today's tarot card designs are multitudinous. They are thematic and reflect modern specific trends. Some have dreamlike images, gothic images, sexual images, religious, or philosophical imagery.

There are decks for every kind of reader and every kind of person seeking a reading. Nevertheless, the Rider-Waite deck of 1910 is still considered the authoritative standard. It is the deck that everyone around the world—who knows about tarot—understands.

Rider-Waite is the only deck we will talk about in this book. We will look at the imagery and symbolism of those cards, because regardless of what deck you ultimately end up using, all tarot decks, if they are really tarot, have similar characteristics, and they all have the same type and number of cards.

The tarot deck is a 78-card deck consisting of two parts: a *Major Arcana* and a *Minor Arcana*. The word "arcana" is a noun that simply means "secrets" or "mysteries." In the case of the tarot, it means occult secrets. And it is possible to do a reading with just one or the other, but usually readings are done with both arcanas intermingled. The Major Arcana is a set of 22 independent cards. The Fool is the 0 card, and The World is the 21st card.

Cards of the Major Arcana

0. The Fool	XI. Justice
I. The Magician	XII. The Hanged Man
II. The High Priestess	XIII. Death
III. The Empress	XIV. Temperance
IV. The Emperor	XV. The Devil
V. The Hierophant	XVI. The Tower
VI. The Lovers	XVII. The Star
VII. The Chariot	XVIII. The Moon
VIII. Strength	XIX. The Sun
IX. The Hermit	XX. Judgment
X. Wheel of Fortune	XXI. The World

The Minor Arcana, on the other hand, is structured like regular playing cards. The Minor Arcana consists of 56 cards. There are four suits, and 14 cards in each suit. The suits include:

Wands

Pentacles

Cups

Swords

Each suite has 4 face cards: a King, Queen, Knight and Page. Each suit also has 10 pip cards: Ace through 10. Sometimes the Major Arcana is called the "trump cards" and the Minor Arcana is called the "court cards." Within the court cards are the face cards and the pip cards.

Playing cards and tarot cards are really the same thing. Modern playing cards, like you might see in a deck of Bicycle® playing cards, are a derivative of tarot cards. In the beginning, tarot cards were used for games and gambling. Later they became an instrument of divination and thus playing cards branched off from the tarot deck. The playing cards were for games and gambling, the tarot cards were for occult divination.

Modern playing cards have different suits, but they mean the same thing.

Hearts = Cups	Clubs = Wands
Spades = Swords	Diamonds = Pentacles

In modern playing cards, the Jack replaces the Knight and there is no Page. Also, there is no Major Arcana; there is only the Minor Arcana. Thus, a limited tarot reading can be done using regular playing cards. For instance a 9 of Spades has the same divinatory meaning as the 9 of Swords in a tarot deck.

Of course with playing cards, you do not have the imagery to assist you with the symbolic message associated with each card. You would have to already know what each card of the Minor Arcana looks like in order to use playing cards as their replacement.

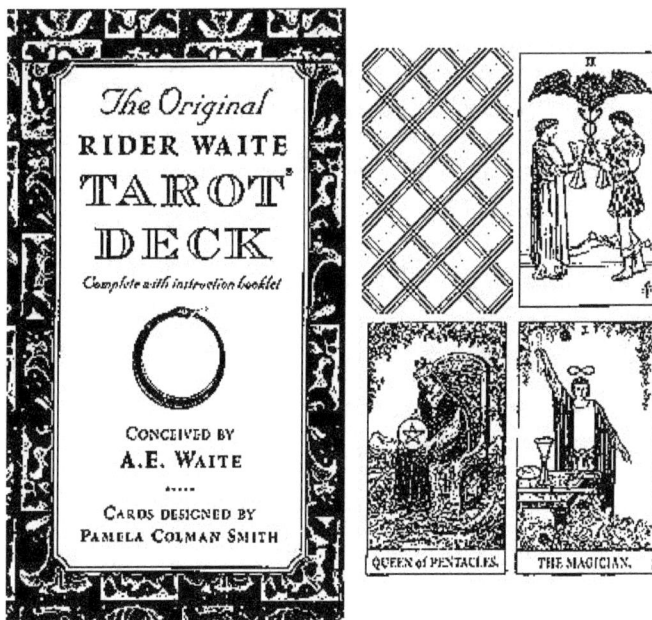

The Rider-Waite Tarot deck. The most popular version published in the world is this one by U.S. Games Systems Inc.®

History of the Tarot Deck

Some people believe the tarot cards are very old. Some believe they only came to the fore in the early 20th century. Both theories are correct. The standard tarot cards we use today, the Rider-Waite deck, was created in 1910. However, *cartomancy*, that is telling the future with playing cards, stretches back centuries.

The imagery of the Rider-Waite deck is also centuries old, but the symbolism of those images, especially those of the Major Arcana, stretch back even further, thousands of years in fact, and owe a great deal to astrology, Ancient Egyptian mysticism, and Ancient Hebrew Kabbalah. Thus the symbolism of tarot is as old as the collective unconsciousness of mankind itself.

Below is a timeline leading up to the Rider-Waite Tarot deck, the standard tarot deck used for divination:

1392: Printing of the *Gringonneur* deck owned by Charles VI of France. The earliest tarot cards that are still in existence. There are only 17 of them left. Though somewhat controversial, this deck is thought to be located in the Bibliotheque Nationale, in Paris.

1422: The earliest surviving full deck painted by an Italian artist named Bonifacio Bembo. It is also known as the Visconti deck, named after the then Duke of Milan.

1450: A sermon is given by a Franciscan friar in Italy denouncing the Major Arcana as an invention of the Devil. Most likely this is because they were used for gambling.

1540: A book entitled *The Oracles of Francesco Marcolino da Forlì* is the first record prescribing the use of playing cards for simple method of divination.

1770: Jean-Baptiste Alliette (aka Etteilla) publishes the Divinatory meanings for the Major and Minor Arcanas. His deck was the first to be made available to the public. It was the first deck specifically meant for divination.

1781: Antoine Court de Gebelin argues that the Major Arcana is Ancient Egyptian in origin containing the wisdom of Toth, the Egyptian god of written knowledge.

1885: Bicycle® playing cards were published.

1910: Rider-Waite Deck is commissioned by Arthur Edward Waite, who wrote *The Key to the Tarot.* He was a prominent member of the occult group, Golden Dawn. The artist was Pamela Colman Smith. William Rider & Son, based in London, was the first publisher of the cards.

Pamela Smith   Arthur Waite

1942: Arthur Edward Waite dies. He was born in Brooklyn, New York, in 1857.

1957: Pamela Colman Smith dies in obscurity.

1971: Tarot cards reemerge when Stuart R. Kaplan, owner of U.S. Games Systems® re-discovers the Rider-Waite deck and gains the rights to publish it.

2016: Over 1,600 different tarot decks are in print throughout the world.

3

Choosing Your Tarot Deck

———————— ● ● ————————

Many newcomers to the practice of tarot reading want to know how to obtain their first deck of cards. Which is the right kind? How do I know which deck is the right deck for me? The answer to these questions is made no simpler by the fact that there are now in print over 1600 different brands of tarot cards.

The first thing you must understand is that you will need two different decks. The first deck must be the Rider -Waite tarot deck. It is the standard throughout the world. Every tarot reader may have their own preference and choose all manner of different decks, but all tarot readers will agree that the Rider-Waite deck is the gold standard. It is the deck to which all others are compared.

Fortunately, a deck of Rider-Waite tarot cards is very easy to obtain. They are available at Barnes and Noble®

bookstores, at Walmart.com®, and of course Amazon.com®. Just search for Rider-Waite tarot cards and it will come right up. At the time of this writing, such a deck offered by Amazon.com® costs between $13-15. The $15 dollar "pack" comes with a booklet by A.E. Waite that describes the meaning of the tarot cards.

Unfortunately, very few people actually agree with A.E. Waite's descriptions of the cards. Some of the definitions and keywords he gives don't match very well with most reader's psychic impression of the cards when they view them. And you have to keep in mind that though he had Pamela Colman Smith paint the images that are on the Rider-Waite deck, he didn't invent those images. They have been around for centuries; therefore, he is no more an expert on their meaning than any other sorcerer. But we will get more into this in a later chapter.

The point is that whether you buy the pack or the deck, either one gives you an identical set of cards that are large, sturdy, and intended for years of use. I have a few decks of Rider-Waite cards I've collected over the years, and they are all still in great shape.

Rider-Waite is the deck you will learn tarot with. This is the deck we use in this book to discuss the symbolism of the illustrations. So, the first thing you need to do is obtain a deck of Rider-Waite cards, assuming you don't already have one. Once you have them, there is nothing you can't do in tarot.

Of course, eventually, you may find the Rider-Waite deck to be a bit sterile, psychically speaking. A lot of people do. I find the deck to be too academic. For me, it's like using a student's violin. It works, but it's not really the instrument you want when you move up to the orchestra. You want something you feel connected to personally. That's why there are so many other decks published with all manner of themes from wildlife, to gothic imagery, to sexual imagery, to LGBT imagery, classical mediaeval imagery, or renaissance images. Just about any theme you can imagine, there's a tarot deck that uses it.

All these alternate tarot decks have the same cards as the Rider-Waite. They may call them something different, like the way my deck calls a "page" a "princess," but they all equate to the Rider-Waite deck in some fashion. You will want to find this kind of personal deck for yourself. This will be the deck that inspires you the most. This will be *your* deck.

Some people say that you have to have your *personal* deck gifted to you for it to be real and for it to work. I heartily disagree. In fact, I believe the opposite is true. I have been given lots of tarot decks over the years, but *I* have chosen the one I call my own. There is no one who can tell you what kind of deck you should have for your personal deck other than yourself. Therefore, actually shopping for it and obtaining it by yourself and for yourself is highly important, in my opinion.

Finding Your Personal Deck

Go to Google "Images" and type in "various tarot decks." You will get a huge assortment of the tarot decks that are out there. It's better to do this with a full screen. I can do it on my phone, because I have a large phone, but it is easier to see them and enlarge them on a full screen.

Scroll through the images without really looking at each one. Try instead to look at them collectively. Then when you see something that "catches your eye" stop and look at that one more closely. Write down what kind it is, and continue scrolling.

There's no hurry. You have your Rider-Waite deck, so you're not prevented from doing tarot. You want to get the selection of a personal deck right. Even if you collect lots of decks, you will still always have your personal favorite. That personal favorite is what you're looking for now, so take your time with this.

When you have four or five decks written down, go back and study each one separately. You may want to look on Amazon.com® and read the product description, and you may want to search on Google for any information on that particular deck. Try to narrow your preferences down to just two.

Look at each one of two remaining decks. Which one has imagery that makes you look deeper into it? Which one gives you a sense of wonder? Which one makes you stare at it longer than the others? That's the deck for you. It's really that simple.

Some Precautionary Advice

There are some decks that are just downright silly: tarot decks based on Sponge Bob, The Simpsons, action hero tarot decks, Flintstones tarot, etc. Avoid these decks. I find it highly unlikely that anyone who appreciates the dark sorcery that tarot is would ever want such a deck in the first place, except perhaps to collect it for fun. They would certainly never use it in readings. Tarot is serious business, so always treat it that way. It can be interesting, even entertaining, but it should never be taken lightly.

Also realize that in order to call it a tarot deck, it has to have the cards that are in a tarot deck. It has to have the Major Arcana and the Minor Arcana represented, and the symbols have to be at least similar to the Rider-Waite deck. The 9 of Swords, for instance, should have a figure showing regretful worry with nine swords. The Star card should have a nude figure pouring out water into a body of water and also onto the land with a prominent star showing. If the standard Rider-Waite imagery isn't the main theme of the cards, it's not really a tarot deck.

Angel cards are not tarot cards. Crystal cards are not tarot cards. Even though playing cards can represent the Minor Arcana, they can only do so abstractly. If you lay the 9 of Spades, that's the same as the 9 of Swords, but you still have to know what the actual 9 of Swords from the Rider-Waite deck looks like in order to use the playing card as a substitute.

So, now is the time to go and get your Rider-Waite deck and choose your personal deck. In a later chapter, we will look at how to bind your personal deck to yourself in order to make it yours entirely, but that can't be done until you have your cards.

The cost of the cards is typically not that much; try not to let it be a consideration when choosing your deck. It's not like buying a car. The Illuminati deck I own is pretty expensive, and yet as of the time of this writing, it only costs about $35. Once you have your cards, you will have them for many years, maybe for life. Later on, we'll cover how to care for your cards to ensure they last a long time, so whatever the expense, it's probably worth it in the long run. What's most important is that you have a deck that really inspires your psychic sense of divination.

4

Interpreting the Cards

———————● ●——————

We will examine now what each card means. In this chapter, we'll look at the symbolism within the card itself, as well as provide some keywords that help us to easily remember what the card means.

Keep in mind, however, that even though I'm giving you the standard symbolic representations and keywords, there really are no "official" meanings for any of the cards. The cards are a psychic crutch, and when examined in a spread, they provide a psychic story. That story *is* the reading.

Sometimes, it's not clear what the cards are saying. In that case, the standard meanings can be relied upon. If a psychic story is not coming through, that is an indication to go with the standard meanings. Also, learning the standard meanings is kind of like learning the basic chords of a song. You learn the chords, you practice the chords, but the beauty and the art is all in how you fill in in the chords with grace notes, progressions, etc. It's the same with tarot. Let the standard meanings ground you, but then reach out and feel for the psychic story.

A good example of this would be a reading I did for a young woman who asked, "Will I be happily married again?" The cards that came up after a full ritualistic reading were the Queen of Swords, the King of Swords and the World card.

Now, each one of these cards has a standard meaning and associated keywords, but the psychic story was clear, and I never even consulted the standard meanings. Here was a queen and a king together and the World card. The psychic story was clear: "You will have a grand wedding and supremely happy marriage, and you will have everything you want from it!"

Nevertheless, as a student, you must become familiar with the standard meanings. They form your academic understanding. They provide a platform for you to stand on before you dive off into and interpretation. It can be said that a true tarotist knows the standard meanings, and she knows them so well that she never has to use them.

THE
MAJOR ARCANA

Introduction

The Major Arcana is the Grand Set in the tarot cards. These cards indicate a stronger fate than the Minor Arcana. The Major Arcana consists of twenty-two cards, and each one has ancient symbols associated with it.

Carl Jung, the famous psychoanalyst, the most famous student of Sigmund Freud, believed that the Major Arcana contained the symbols of the archetypes of the human collective mind. In other words, the symbols within these cards are understood on fundamental, perhaps even a spiritual level, by all human beings.

It is said that a reading that contains a large number of Major Arcana cards is a more fated reading. In other words, it may be a reading that does not allow for a lot of control or change based on free will. A reading that has all Major Arcana cards means that the reader or the querent may not be able to change what is foretold, or if they do choose to change that fate, it may require a great deal of effort.

This solid fate aspect of the Major Arcana is sometimes feared, but on the other hand it is sometimes desired, and in fact a reading can be done using only the Major Arcana. An example of such a situation might be when someone wants to make an investment and needs a clear go-no-go indication. Below is a list of the 22 Major Arcana cards:

0. The Fool	XI. Justice
I. The Magician	XII. The Hanged Man
II. The High Priestess	XIII. Death
III. The Empress	IVX. Temperance
IV. The Emperor	XV. The Devil
V. The Hierophant	XVI. The Tower
VI. The Lovers	XVII. The Star
VII. The Chariot	XVIII. The Moon
VIII. Strength	XIX. The Sun
IX. The Hermit	XX. Judgment
X. Wheel of Fortune	XXI. The World

Let's look at each of the cards in the Major Arcana in turn. Don't be afraid to make your own notes on these cards regarding your own personal impressions or intuitions about their meaning. Remember, the standard meanings are a guide, but your psychic impressions matter, too.

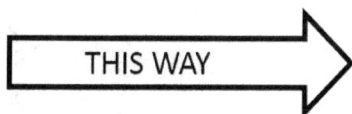

THIS WAY →

THE FOOL .

0. The Fool

Description

The figure is walking with his knapsack. This can indicate travelling or moving on, but he is headed blindly over a cliff ignoring the warning of the dog (a spirit guide or familiar), because he is preoccupied with lovely thoughts, not ever expecting anything bad to happen.

Interpretation

The start of a journey into the unknown. A warning to wake up and be careful. A call to a more carefree life. It can mean a person looking for a fresh start or a need to move on beyond a situation or relationship.

Keywords

- Danger ahead
- Journey
- Free of worry
- Ignorance
- New adventures
- Starting out
- Moving on
- Innocence

THE MAGICIAN.

1. The Magician

Description

Here we see a figure that represents the ability for the human mind to change reality. He is a witch, and even though the figure is male, it equally applies to females when the card shows up in a reading. In one hand, he points to the astral realm; the other points to the earth, indicating "As above, so below." Infinity is above his head indicating the eternal nature of the individual human mind. Around his waist is a snake biting it's own tail, another sign of eternity. On the table before him are the suits of the Minor Arcana: A wand, a sword, a cup, and a pentacle. This indicates the power of the human will and intent over the fatalistic forces of the universe.

Interpretation

The power of will. The magical ability of the querent. The astral realm. A warning of magic being used against you. The evolving human being. The presence of a spirit guide. It can also symbolize psi ability overall or a unique gift for focusing those areas of the mind that utilize psi energies.

Keywords

- Eternity
- Magical ability
- Presence of magic
- Human will
- Psi potential
- Psi energy

THE HIGH PRIESTESS

2. The High Priestess

Description

Here a sorceress sits between the mighty pillars of the temple of Solomon, a temple constructed by the 72 demons of the Goetia in the Lesser Key of Solomon. The B and J stand for Boaz and Jachin and mean "strength that is established." A tapestry of pomegranates is draped behind her indicating the fruits of labor, the attainment of spiritual wealth. The pillars are both black and white showing that the figure is the ruler of right and wrong. She has the phases of the moon on her head (witchcraft) and the crescent moon at her feet (Islam). She has a cross on her chest (Christianity), and the Torah on her lap (Judaism); thus she possesses great wisdom of both the world and the astral realm, philosophies, religions, beliefs, and yet she transcends them all. She rules them all.

Interpretation

Transcending right and wrong. The control of demonic forces, the manipulator of deluded minds, the power of sorcery, the priest or priestess of all religions. vast occult wisdom, great astral understanding

Keywords:

- Understanding

- Wisdom

- Sorcery

- Right and wrong

- Transcendence

- Spiritual leadership

- Teaching spiritual things

THE EMPRESS.

3. The Empress

Description

Here a beautiful woman sits leisurely on an outdoor throne next to a flowing river. She wears a loose gown decorated with fruit, a crown of stars and holds a scepter with a moon on the top of it. At her feet is a heart-shaped plaque with the symbol of Venus on it. She exudes woman hood and the feminine possibility of fertility. She even seems to command it as she stares out at us.

Interpretation

This card appears to symbolize the feminine. It not only represents physical fertility, but also creativity and beauty. This is the card of artistic success as well as pregnancy. It is a very positive card typically, but must always be considered in the context in which it appears. The flowing river represents creativity; the heart represents love and beauty. The surrounding lush forest and the grass represent bountiful crops, or anything else that we might try to "grow." The scepter she holds represents the magick used to create love, fertility, and creativity, and even prosperity by extension.

Keywords

- Femininity

- Beauty

- Creativity

- Mother

- Fertility

- Raw talent

- Pregnancy

- Bountiful harvests

- Prosperity

THE EMPEROR.

4. The Emperor

Description

A magnificent king sits on a stone throne (a throne that will never pass away). He holds a scepter in one hand and an orb in the other. Ram's heads are on his armrests and the back of the throne. The rams represent Aries (symbolic of force and power). Behind him sits a stone mountain range and a river, the most powerful symbols of nature. The king has a long beard implying wisdom and experience. He wears armor which represents impenetrability.

Interpretation

This card represents authority in all its forms. It is the image of the father, of power, of command, and ultimate decision-making. It can be seen as an image of the Divine ruler of the universe, or as the law of the land. It also can symbolize the power of human will--which is greater than the fatalistic forces of the universe. The mountain range in the background is solid, like granite, and symbolizes the Divine Right to rule or a powerbase that is backed up by the very logic of nature itself.

Keywords

- Father

- God

- Authority

- Law

- Divine Right

- Leadership

- Power

- Wisdom

- Logical choice

THE HIEROPHANT

5. The Hierophant

Description

The word "hierophant" means a person, especially a priest in Ancient Greece who interprets sacred mysteries or esoteric principles. In some tarot decks, the Hierophant is called the Pope. Notice that it shows a figure on a throne between two pillars, traditionally interpreted as right and wrong. At his feet are the Keys of Heaven and two subordinate priests kneel before him to receive his blessing. He wears a triple crown (called a "mitre") which indicates the kingdom of heaven, and holds a crosier, a triple cross, which indicates the trinity.

Interpretation

This card represents the delusional spell of religion. It can stand for the concept of morality or right and wrong. The keys are what keep people spiritual bound to the wisdom he proclaims. This is the card of social expectations and a need to conform. It tells us not to step out of line. It tells us to relinquish our spiritual evolution to a religious system. Or, more positively, it tells us to "do the right thing." It can also be said to be calling one to be their own hierophant.

Keywords

- Morality
- Religion
- Religious delusion
- Spiritual captivity
- Personal religion
- Right actions
- Repentance
- Christianity

THE LOVERS.

6. The Lovers

Description

A nude woman and man stand under the overshadow of a great angel. The man stands in front of the Tree of Life, and the woman stands in front of the Tree of Knowledge. A serpent winds around the Tree of Knowledge. The sun is at its zenith above the angel and a barren hill is in the background.

Interpretation

This card has many meanings. Mostly it means marriage or relationships between lovers. The barren mountain serves to show us that such relationships are needed to transform the earth into a populated place. The Angel is blessing the union of lovers and hence the card also represents unions of all kinds. The sun which empowers the angel signifies the Divine plane to separate people by gender and thus have to overcome much in order to find unity. The man and woman obviously symbolize Adam and Eve who are without clothes and so we see a sinless nature, or innocence about them. We also see an image that suggest the very foundation of human evolution, and with the angel and religious presentation, we could assume that's primarily a spiritual evolution.

Keywords

- Union

- Marriage

- Love

- Relationships

- Spiritual Evolution

- Human purpose

- Innocence

- Primordial Humankind

THE CHARIOT.

7. The Chariot

Description

The charioteer is a prince, a member of royalty, but not royalty of this world. He is royalty on the astral plane. See how he resides under a canopy of stars, which symbolize the astral realm See how crescent moons are on the shoulders of his armor, indicating magic. Magic in this case being mental will and intent applied through the powers of spirit. See how the sphinxes power the chariot, one white and one black. This indicates his mastery over the dark and light forces of the spiritual realm.

Interpretation

When this card appears in a reading one might think of an old soul, an elevated favorite of the greater spirits of the astral realm. This is one who will not reincarnate. It also indicates a need to gain mastery of one's magical abilities, to focus on being a citizen of the spirit rather than of the world. It also means will and mastery, in general, and traditionally implies victory or triumph in a situation.

Keywords

- Will

- Intent

- Magical abilities

- Mastery

- Victory

- Triumph

- Astral realm

STRENGTH.

8. Strength

Description

In this card we see a woman dressed in white holding the jaws of a lion. Above her head is the symbol of infinity indicating the eternal nature of human consciousness, giving it dominance over the physical non-spiritual world. We see a woman who is unafraid to interact with the animal level within the world, and yet she is not angry or violent with it. She is calm and appears somewhat caring. Nevertheless, she is in charge and of a higher caste than the bestial inhabitants of the world around her.

Interpretation

Lions often represent kings. Therefore, this card indicates that the advanced spirit is stronger than an earthly king. This card praises the human spirit, which is eternal and places it over the physical environment. Moreover, it indicates that true strength resides in our spiritual nature, not in our bestial nature. It is also shows why civilization within the natural world must suppress the individual human spirit, because nothing is as strong as the untethered human spirit.

When this card appears in a reading, it means spiritual strength. It can also mean physical strength depending on the context of the question. It means standing up to the world through the strength of spirit. It also means having the ability to dominate in a situation.

Keywords

- Domination
- Strength
- Spiritual strength
- Spiritual dominance
- The spiritual caste
- Eternal nature

9. The Hermit

Description

This card shows a figure in a hooded black cloak holding a staff and a lantern. The staff symbolizes a firm commitment, and the black cloak represents the occult nature of the figure. The figure is old with a white beard and appears to be looking down. The white beard represents wisdom, and his downward glance indicates contemplation. The ground around him is snowy, and the landscape is bleak. This symbolizes an empty astral plane, and since there is nothing else in the card, and he is isolated, we can assume this is his undeveloped astral plane. The light within the lantern is illuminated with a 6-point star, the symbol of Solomon, which also points to wisdom. Beyond the wasteland is a mountain range in the distance, but it is also covered with snow. This represents the vastness of the astral plane.

Interpretation

The Hermit card indicates that one must look inward and contemplate the spiritual wisdom they have gained. It also indicates someone who has not developed their astral plane and is thus contemplating a return to the physical world as a guide. Thus this card represents a spirit guide. The glowing lantern tells us that a light is shining in the darkness, and this may be applied to the querent or to the light a spirit guide brings to us. This card may also indicate the decision to make a religious journey away from the community of religion and into the hidden realms of the occult.

Keywords

- Occult

- Isolation

- Introspection

- The astral plane

- Spirit guides

- Light in the dark

WHEEL of FORTUNE.

10. Wheel of Fortune

Description

The first thing we notice is a wheel with writing on it. It says "TAROT," and then the Hebrew letters in-between spell out YHWH or the name of God. Both are part of a spinning wheel representing the underlying chaos of the universe, which is duplicated in the shuffling of the tarot deck.

In each corner of the card is a figure sitting in the heavenly realms. Each one represents an astrological sign and thus a primary fatalistic force within the universe. The angel represents Aquarius; the eagle represents Scorpio; the Bull represents Taurus, and the lion represents Leo.

These four fatalistic forces are shown as writers, and as such, they represent the forces that write order into the universe from the chaos of the spinning wheel.

Rotating on the outside of the wheel are three symbolic figures: a sphinx with a sword (representing triumph, endurance, and understanding), a Typhon (representing dread and misfortune), and the Ancient Egyptian god, Anibus (representing death and transition to the afterlife). As the wheel spins around by chance, the fatalistic forces write our destines, and this results in alternating periods of fortune and misfortune.

Interpretation

When this card shows up in a reading it means a chance occurrence is about to unfold. It may mean that the querent needs to understand that fatalistic forces are at work in his or her life. It could mean they need to take a chance or that they are taking too many chances. It may also mean that order is forming from chaos in their life. Another interpretation may be that they need to start using their capabilities to write their own destiny rather than having it written for them.

Keywords

- Taking Chances

- Fatalistic forces

- Gambling

- Uncertainty

- Creating order

11. Justice

Description

Here we see a robed figure sitting on a throne holding a scale in one hand and a sword in the other. The scales represent equity, and the sword represents truth and finality, and perhaps even punishment. Notice the figure is seated between two pillars, which are the pillars of Solomon's temple, which indicate wisdom. It's also important to notice the robe and the crown, because these represent royalty, and that tells us that the matters of this card are exalted and intended for a more refined evolution.

Interpretation

This card often represents decisions. For instance in the past position it may represent a decision that was made in the past that is now affecting the present. Also the card represents the law: law enforcement, lawyers, courthouses, legal matters, etc. It also represents what is fair and equitable and balances of all kinds: balance in relationships, balance in emotions, and balance in life. In that regard, it is closely associated with the astrological constellation of Libra.

Keywords

- Law

- Balance

- Justice

- Equality

- Decisions

- Fairness

THE HANGED MAN.

12. The Hanged Man

Description

Here we see a figure hanging from a tree limb upside down by one foot. It depicts a *pittura infamante* (pronounced [pit'tuːra iɱfa'mante]), a shameful image of a traitor being punished in a manner common at the time for traitors in Italy. His other leg is crossed behind the suspended leg, and his hands are behind his back. There is a halo around his head and he seems to be at peace with his situation. The card is strange in that it seems the figure is in some kind of peril, but then it almost seems acrobatic, as if the man is showing off. This card is often considered the martyrs card.

Interpretation

This card symbolizes martyrdom or self-sacrifice. It represents service over self and the idea of the good being punished for something they should not be punished for. It also represents being stalled or hung up, and this may mean that a decision needs to be postponed or an event will be held up. Another interpretation says that one is strong enough to bear the sufferings in their life, just as the figure seems to be peacefully enduring his predicament.

Keywords

- Perseverance

- Long suffering

- Martyrdom

- Self-sacrifice

- The Common Good

- Postponement

- Doing for others

DEATH.

13. Death

Description

The figure on the white horse is a skeleton in black armor. He is carrying a flag, and below him is a dead man in a king's robe with his family (a woman and child) apparently mourning his death, and a priest giving the last rights. In the background is the sun setting behind two towers as if at dusk. Interestingly, one really doesn't know if the sun is setting or rising. And the horse the dark figure is riding is white, which is a symbol of good and also of transition. The flower on the flag represents nature and tells us that death comes in the name of nature.

Interpretation

First off, the card represents death, death in any manner of anything. It is the end of a thing or of a situation. It's the force of nature that brings about the end of the physical. It represents termination. It represents a natural end to things. The sun, however, being indeterminate as to whether it is rising or setting indicates the process of reincarnation. The king lying on the ground tells us that nothing and no one is spared. It can also mean defeat, and it is often interpreted to mean transition.

Keywords

- Death

- Finality

- Natural end

- Transition

- Reincarnation

- Termination

- Defeat

14. Temperance

Description

In this card we see an angel pouring water from one cup into another. This indicates the changing of moods and emotions; it means emotional liability. One of its feet is in a pond of water (emotionalism), and the other is on dry land (rationalism). In the background the sun is indeterminate as to whether it is rising or setting. This indicates the elevation and escalation of mood and the depressiveness or darkening of mood.

Interpretation

This card represents trying to find balance with the emotions. It represents the discipline of being neither apathetic nor overly upset. It indicates a rational approach to things and mental stability. It can also mean a problem with mental stability, and it represents a return to emotional balance.

Keywords

- Emotional upset

- Rationalism

- Balance

- Mental stability

- Grounding

- Seeing both sides

- Understanding

- Waiting

- Patience

THE DEVIL .

15. The Devil

Description

Here we see the Baphomet, a traditional symbol of the devil. He has a pentagram between his horns on the top of his head indicating witchcraft or the occult. His outstretched wings are those of a bat representing a creature of the darkness. Before him are two naked figures, male and female, and they are bound to him by a chain and collar. They are his captives and his slaves. Notice they also have small horns on their head and tails indicating they are his offspring. In his left hand he holds a burning path representing the left hand path or the path of darkness.

Interpretation

This is a card of bondage to any and all things that prevent human freedom, especially human spiritual and moral freedom. It can also represent Satan. It can represent human desire, especially those of a taboo nature. Moreover it can represent addictions of any kind. Or it can represent being tied to an unwanted situation. From a religious perspective it can represent sins of all kinds. And even a cursory glance fills one with a sense of danger or perhaps a warning. See how the devil is there with his hand up, as if warning that one is approaching something bad?

Keywords

- Satan

- Bondage

- Addiction

- Slavery

- Bad Situation

- Sexual Desire

- Taboo Things

- Sin

- Danger

- Warning

THE TOWER.

16. The Tower

Description

Here we see a tower being hit by lightning with a crown blowing off the top of it. It's on fire, and terrified people are falling from it. This is the most ominous card in the tarot deck. It rarely indicates anything good. The tower is crumbling from the top down, and smoke is billowing from it.

Interpretation

This card represents disaster, and bad things that are to happen. It's bad luck. It represents a bad idea or a destructive path, especially a self-destructive path. It represents failure, tragedy, death, and a dramatic end. It can mean disaster in a lesser degree, as well, such as a fight or argument, or a mistake at work. It also can mean the end of a rulership, or the change of authority, or a lost election.

Keywords

- Disaster

- Destruction

- Death

- Fights and arguments

- Bad luck

- Tragic ends

- The end of a reign

- Overthrow

THE STAR.

17. The Star

Description

Here we see a nude figure pouring water from jugs, one in each hand. From one, she pours into a pond and from the other she pours onto the land. Above her is a star-filled sky with a large yellow start centered above her. The bird in the tree in the background symbolizes the flight of the soul into the heavenly realms. The woman is naked to symbolize the true nature of a person. The water spilling onto the land is bringing life in the form of green grass and budding plants.

Interpretation

Universally this card represents hope or a new hope; however it has other meanings as well. It represents the nature of humanity with the universe, Divine favor from above, astral travel, and the transference of spirit from the astral realm to the physical realm by means of a natural human, thus it is the symbol of a medium. It is also a symbol of the emotions in general.

Keywords

- Hope

- Mediumship

- Divine Favor

- Universal Harmony

- Human Nature

- The Astral Realm

- Astral Travel

- Emotions

THE MOON.

18. The Moon

Description

In this card, the moon is looking down grimly toward the earth. The moon is considered the great malefic. It is a symbol of dark emotions in the tarot deck. It can also represent bad luck. It is positioned between two towers, which symbolize the constructs of man or the situations we create for ourselves. There are dogs barking at it. They represent anxiety and stress and mental instability, think "barking mad." From the pond before them a crayfish crawls up onto the land onto a road that leads off into the distance far beyond the towers. This is a symbol of human evolution through the pains of adversity.

Interpretation

This is the card of mental illness, mental stress, anxiety, and even psychosis or paranoia. It is the card of hard luck and adversity. It is also the card of learning via hard experience, and the card of evolving through hard times. It can represent negative emotions or act as a warning against bad things to come. It can be seen as a bad omen.

Keywords

- Mental Issues
- Stress
- Evolution
- Adversity
- Bad Luck
- Night of the Soul
- Emotional Upset
- Being Wrong
- Negativity

THE SUN .

19. The Sun

Description

A naked child, representing youth and new beginnings, rides upon a white horse which symbolizes hope and purity with the bright sun over his head. The sun is considered a symbol of power, energy, life, vitality, and good fortune overall. In the child's left hand is a red pennant and sunflowers are growing behind him. These represent the spring and new life, or a birth.

Interpretation

This card typically represents the start of something good. It is often indicative of pregnancy or birth. It is generally a good-luck card, and it specifically means a new beginning. It can mean a fresh start and a return to energy, vitality and health. In general, it indicates happiness and mental wellbeing. It often heralds the start of something good

Keywords

- Mental health
- Happiness
- Energy
- New Start
- The Beginning
- Pregnancy
- Birth
- Babies
- Joy
- Pleasure
- Health
- Good Fortune

JUDGEMENT.

20. Judgement

Description

Here we see an angel blowing a trumpet. The trumpet signifies truth, specifically truth about ourselves. On the trumpet is a flag with a red cross. This may have had Christian origins, but it's not really a Christian cross or flag. Nevertheless, it does represent righteousness or doing the right thing, specifically it represents a kind of spiritual evolution through correct behavior or following the correct path. Below the angel are people rising up from their graves to receive what is being given and what they have earned, both good and bad. This is a message indicating our existence after death and the acceptance of what we've earned after living a life here on earth.

Interpretation

This card tells us that we must do what is necessary for spiritual growth and evolution. It speaks specifically about judgment or discernment, but it has afterlife implications, such as karma, or rewards and punishments. It reminds us that someone is watching and judging us, both divinely, or it could mean that we are being judged by someone here on earth, depending on the context of the question and the position of the card in the spread. In a lesser context, it could mean an evaluation such as a test in school or an evaluation at work.

Keywords

- The Right Thing

- Spiritual Evolution

- Karma

- Discernment

- The Afterlife

- Eternal Life

- Judgment

- Evaluations

- Tests

- Worthiness

THE WORLD.

21. The World

Description

A nude figure is encircled by a reef within the heavens. The reef is a circle that indicates a monistic wholeness. In each of her hands are wands, indicating the ability to make decisions, cause events, and manipulate her world. At each corner of the card is one of the four astrological symbols, the Lion is Leo, a fire sign; the Bull is Taurus, an earth sign; the Man is Aquarius, an air sign; and the Eagle is Scorpio, a water sign. These signs represent the four elements of the physical world. Overall, this this card represents the universe and humankind's place within it. The figure is draped in a purple pennant representing royalty, or a elevated class distinction.

Interpretation

This card can represent the universe and all that that means. It can also represent having "everything." It represents the forces of nature, as well as a person's place or purpose within the world. It represents our control in life, and perhaps the love of the Divine for its own creation and manifestation as a human being. It can also represent the mind of the Divine, or consciousness itself. It is generally considered a positive card.

Keywords

- The Divine
- Natural forces
- Monism
- Purpose
- Control
- Attainment
- Good disposition
- Consciousness
- Class distinction
- All things
- The physical realm

THE

MINOR ARCANA

Introduction

The Major Arcana is said to express global ideas and universal themes. It has cards like Judgement, The World, The Emperor, etc. The Minor Arcana, on the other hand, relates to specific areas of life. It concerns the actions we take, the emotions we feel, the way we think, and the material things we acquire and own.

The total tarot deck is 78 cards. The Major Arcana has 22 of them; the Minor Arcana has the other 56, and it contains the following suits: Wands, Cups, Swords, and Pentacles. Different decks use different nomenclature for some of these suits. Sometimes Pentacles are called Coins; sometimes Wands are called Staffs, but symbolically it's all the same thing. In fact, the Minor Arcana relates to the ordinary playing cards with the Cups being hearts, Swords being spades, Wands being clubs, and Pentacles being Diamonds. Also, each suit of the Minor Arcana has court cards, also known as face cards; they include the King, Queen, Knight, and Page. And each suit also has 10 pip cards (Ace thru 10).

It's important to understand that each suit (Wands, Swords, Cups, Pentacles) represents one of the four astrological elements (Fire, Water, Air, Earth). Wands are Fire, Cups are Water, Swords are Air, and Pentacles are Earth.

Wands, just like Fire, correspond to action and movement. Cups, just like Water, correspond to spirit and emotions. Swords, just like Air, correspond to thought and reason, and Pentacles, just like Earth, correspond to material things and money. So, because these cards relate to the four basic elements of astrology, we find that the cards share a common symbolism with the astrological signs. For instance in astrology Aries is all about action. Aries is a fire sign. Wands are a Fire sign, and consequently Wands are all about action, just like Aries.

Because of this, tarot is considered a sister form of divination to astrology. The difference is that astrology has very specific meanings and therefore requires no psychic ability. Tarot cards, on the other hand, have traditional meanings, but the cards also produce a psychic story in the mind of the reader, and that story can trump the traditional meanings. Thus, reading tarot cards requires some psychic intuition.

Here are some keywords for the suits. These keywords would also be found in the various constellations, houses, and planets of astrology that represent Air, Water, Fire, and Earth.

Wands (Air): action, enthusiasm, movement, masculine, force, passion, decisiveness.

Cups (Water): emotions, intuition, spiritual, flowing, feminine, caring, nurturing.

Swords (Fire): intellect, reason, thought, communications, truth, divination

Pentacles (Earth): money, material goods, possessions, practicality, wealth, abundance

———

In addition, each of the court cards has a general symbolic meaning:

King: male, control, outward expression, authority

Queen: feminine, receptive, inward focus, inward focus,

Knight: youth, extremes, eagerness, high-spirited, energetic

Page: childlike, innocent, playful, pleasure, abandon, adventure

———

As we go through each of these cards, look at the interpretations and keywords, and you'll see how the cards reflect the general symbology of the suits and the faces. And while tarot is a psychic art, and while the psychic story always trumps the standard symbolism, the standard symbolism provides a framework for focusing our psychic intuition.

Ace of Wands

Description

This is the first card of the wands suit. It shows a Divine hand holding a wand and reaching out to the querent. The hand is extending from the ethereal plane into the physical realm. Hills, grass, water, and trees are all in the background. There is also a castle shown sitting on top of a distant hill. Notice that this wand is a living branch and therefore represents life and vitality.

Interpretation

When this card is presented, we first realize that we are dealing with a Divine action; it can also mean a call to action or to make a firm decision. Remember that wands are like Aries in astrology, so this card indicates a primary force or a singular force. It represents passion and fire being handed out or returned to an individual.

Keywords

- Passion
- Force
- Fire
- First things
- Firm decisions
- Authoritative action
- Aries

2 of Wands

Description

Here we see a well-dressed figure standing between two wands. Two wands (two of anything for that matter) often symbolizes a choice. He is holding a globe in his hand (symbolizing his power over a small part of the world, or better yet, *his own* world), and he is gazing out onto the world-at-large. This can be a symbol for finding one's fit.

He stands on the ramparts of a castle wall, which means he has the power or at least the means to choose, and he is apparently looking out to sea. The sea usually means vast spirituality or the Divine, so this tells us the choice he is making is of great importance.

Interpretation

Typically, this card stands for planning an action. Getting ready to take the world. It could mean a graduation from school, the choice on a career or major in college, or the vision of a future that spurs one to act. It asks, *What can I make of my world? What means do I have to make a life for myself?*

Keywords

- Planning

- Choosing

- Contemplating

- Creating a future

- Getting ready to act

- Figuring out the best way

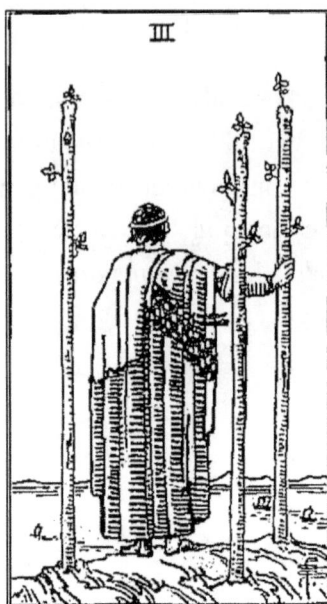

3 of Wands

Description

Here a figure is dressed in royal accruement; this symbolizes a wealth of ability. He is standing on a hilltop
overlooking the sea, and this symbolizes the power of his
vision. In one hand he holds a wand, and behind him are
two others. The other two wands are firmly planted in the
ground indicating significant resolve. On the water below
are three ships heading out to sea, and the figure appears
to be watching them.

Interpretation

This card means that one has set plans into motion and is watching them unfold. It represents taking an action as opposed to planning one. It represents setting sail on an ocean that leads to the future. Think of casting one's bread upon the water. Here one has made up their mind and acted on it. They've considered multiple avenues and chose one. There is a leadership quality inherent in this card, and thus it can stand for leadership, but it also stands for entrepreneurial ideas.

Keywords

- Taking action

- Setting out

- Beginning

- Leadership

- Entrepreneurialism

- The start

- An adventure begins

4 of Wands

Description

Here we see four wands planted in the ground, symbolizing a firm connection to earth or the material world. There is a merry garland draped between them, symbolizing celebration and good times. In the background, we see two figures reveling in front of a large castle that is behind them. The castle represents a home or a hometown.

Interpretation

This card indicates a celebration or the need for celebration. It is a very positive card in the tarot deck, and it often represents a job well done, or the accomplishment of a goal or a graduation, or a promotion. It can represent happiness or a return to better times. It can also represent the return of anything to its rightful place, or the reunion of the lost with the found. In the cases of war or travel, it can certainly indicate a safe return.

Keywords

- Celebration

- Return

- Coming home

- Graduation

- Promotion

- Finding what has been lost

- Accomplishment

5 of Wands

Description

This is a very simple card. There's nothing in the back-ground, there's no special symbols. It's just five figures all fighting each other with wands. There is strife and anger, and each figure is fighting for his own self-interest. Obviously they are angry and indignant.

Interpretation

This card means strife and conflict. More to the point, however, it means primal self-interest. It also suggests the folly of everyone fighting against each other rather than cooperating. Nothing is being accomplished, and even more, nothing can possibly get accomplished. This is a no-win situation. This card is particularly bad when it comes to business, family, or relationship matters. It is generally considered a negative card in just about any situation; however, its negativity can be mitigated somewhat if it seen as describing the conflict inherent in sporting events.

Keywords

- Self-interest
- Conflict
- War
- Competition
- Lack of team work
- Chaos
- Strife
- Arguments
- Fights
- Sporting Competitions

6 of Wands

Description

In this card, we see a figure wearing a wreath on his head and riding a horse. The wreath symbolizes the status of having made a correct decision or having won a conflict. The horse has a green blanket draped over it indicating ceremony and further reinforcing the idea of a triumph of some sort. The figure on the horse is also holding a wand that has a wreath tied to it. This indicates the achievement of something worthwhile, or a just cause. The other figures in the background are cheering him on, suggesting social status as a result of his victory.

Interpretation

This card has traditionally meant the social or public recognition of some achievement. In one respect, we could see the rider as the one who finally emerges from the conflict we saw with the 5 of Wands. This card is associated with winning a game, a lawsuit, a promotion at work, or achieving some other grand end, such as finishing a writing project or perhaps a work of art.

Keywords

- Achievement
- Winning
- Reward
- Recognition
- Publicity
- Standing out
- Becoming better
- Pride
- Self-satisfaction

7 of Wands

Description

You will notice that the wands, as a suit, as discussed in the introduction to the Minor Arcana, are all about action, decision, passion, and drive—like Aries in astrology. The 7 of Wands is no exception. Here we see a figure using his wand to fight off six other challengers who are all against him. He is standing alone against the world so to speak. There is no particular background, but he is standing precariously on the edge of a cliff, indicating that if he fails, he will fall, perhaps even lose his life. He is in a desperate defiant struggle.

Interpretation

This is the king-of-the-hill card. It means standing your ground. It means fighting for what's important to you. It can mean overwhelming odds, or fighting against overwhelming odds. It can stand for desperation, or dangerous environments. Somewhat neutrally, it can mean defiance, either for the good or the bad.

Keywords

- Fighting

- Defiance

- Desperate struggles

- Standing up

- A cause

- Danger

- Overwhelmed

- Long odds

- Can't fail

- Against the world

- Alone

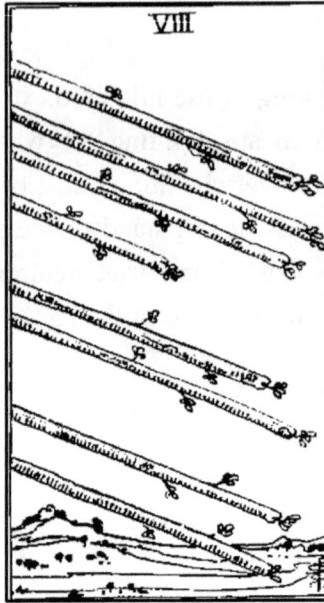

8 of Wands

Description

Here we see eight wands flying through the air, indicating motion at high speed, as well as a kind of freedom. In the background, are a stream and green hills, symbolizing peace, or calm. Sitting on the mountain, in the very back, is a manor house. Houses almost always symbolize the soul of an individual.

Interpretation

The classic interpretation of this card is travel or motion. It is a positive card indicating energy or high speed. It means one is well on their way, that plans are working. It represents freedom from restraint, and this can be taken as a good thing or a bad thing. It can mean the disturbance of calm, and action that disturbs the peace. It is a call to action or a call to strike while the iron is hot.

Keywords

- Motion
- Speed
- Disturbance of peace
- End of calm
- Energy
- Release
- Freedom
- Plans in work

9 of Wands

Description

In this card, we see a figure leaning upon a wand. He is beleaguered, injured, and tired. He is attentive, if not a little paranoid, as he looks for yet another attack to come. Eight other wands stand behind him representing tasks that he's already completed, fights he's already won. Green hills are in the background indicating the world, and indicating that this figure and his condition is the way of the world. The figure seems to have many troubles and issues to deal with.

Interpretation

This card is the card of multiple challenges. It represents the many steps necessary to complete a task. It is the weariness as one approaches the completion of a goal. It also represents being on the lookout for sabotage or mistakes that can ruin everything. It symbolizes giving one's all for the task at hand. It can represent the tasks of management, and it can represent a person who has a great deal of responsibility.

Keywords

- Responsibility

- Beleaguered

- End of a task

- Setbacks

- Street sense

- Weariness

- Concern

- Paranoia

10 of Wands

Description

In the background of this card, we see a castle with a vineyard. This is representative of the soul, as are most dwellings. Toward that castle, we see a figure carrying a bundle of ten wands. These represent all the tasks of daily life we go through in order to maintain our soul and spiritual condition. Notice the figure is carrying this bundle alone without any help. This represents the fact that we must do all the heavy lifting of spiritual development ourselves. No one can help us.

Interpretation

This card is mostly about hard work of any kind. It is a spiritual card, but it can be interpreted for the secular things in life as well. It represents burdens that we need to set down. It represents a journey taken toward the development of the soul, and it represents taking on a lot of issues at once. It represents doing too much as well as having a lot to do. From a spiritual perspective, it can mean hard-learned lessons in life, or sins for that matter.

Keywords

- Hard lessons

- Burdens

- Sins

- Lone work

- Spiritual development

- Excessive work

- Multitasking

- Heavy lifting

- Hard work

PAGE of WANDS.

Page of Wands

Description

Here we see a young man standing with a single wand, and he's gazing upon it. He is dreaming of his plan; he is formulating a creative idea. Notice he is standing in a desert, and there are brown hills in the background. This is undeveloped land; it has potential, but no expression in life as of yet. It's ready to be transformed. Notice the figure has salamanders on his cloak. This is an ancient symbol of transformation.

Interpretation

This card represents the formulation of a dream. It also represents the transformation of the individual into that which is being considered. It represents metamorphosis, and it represents signifying or being signified. It represents initiation or the desire to be initiated. It represents unleashed potential and artistic talents or talents in any field.

Keywords

- Initiation
- Signifying
- Dreaming
- Creativity
- Potential
- Metamorphosis
- Transformation
- Becoming
- Talents
- Undeveloped talent

KNIGHT of WANDS.

Knight of Wands

Description

Here we see a knight, again wearing a cloak with salamanders on it; this is symbolic of transformation. He is dressed in armor, symbolizing resilience, and there are red plumes extending from his helmet and arm, symbolizing fire, which in turn symbolizes passion. He's riding a horse that's obviously full of vigor and energy. This all takes place in a desert with mountains off in the distance. The desert suggests that this is a card not so much concerned with spiritual issues so much as it is with mundane issues. The figure himself is confident and determined, and so this card is generally considered a fortunate card in most spreads.

Interpretation

Traditionally, this card is associated with passion and drive. It can represent taking charge of an idea and running with it enthusiastically. It can represent competence and strength. It can mean being highly proficient at a task or project. This is a person who is good at their job and ready to run with new ideas that spur improvements. Because of its association with passion and force, it can also symbolize lust, lust for another or lust for an idea.

Keywords

- Passion

- Fire

- Drive

- Competence

- Proficiency

- Enthusiasm

- Positive change

- Lust

- Transformation

Queen of Wands

Description

This curious card shows a regal woman sitting on a throne holding a wand. In this, she represents dignity in action, authority, and the ability to choose for her-self. She's holding a sunflower, which symbolizes life and energy, and lions are featured at the top of her headrest as well as on either side of her throne. These lions are large cats that represent strength and courage, but notice there is a strange black cat sitting in front of her. This is a classic symbol of the occult and the darker nature of this figure. Thus we see her as someone who is not completely what she seems to be. This could be a boss figure or a politician. The queen stares off, as if her attention is directed elsewhere, indicating an outward focus or extroversion rather than deep introspection.

Interpretation

This card represents a dominant female figure. This is a leadership card, and is generally considered a positive card. It can represent vitality and life, and good health. It represents taking up command and stepping up to the plate to take charge. It represents street smarts combined with refined wisdom.

Keywords

- Shrewdness
- Leadership
- A boss
- Extroversion
- Vitality
- Health
- In charge
- Courage
- Strength

KING of WANDS

King of Wands

Description

This is the top card in the suit of Wands. For that reason, it represents all the aspects of wands in their purest and strongest form. The King of Wands would be tantamount to Aries in astrology or the element of Fire. Here we see the figure, dressed in fine regalia, representing dignity and entitlement. He is sitting on a throne decorated with lions representing courage and strength. He is wearing a cape with salamander designs and a salamander is on the slab near the throne. Thus we see the power of transformation represented.

Interpretation

This card represents true power, a business leader, a general or commander. It is someone who can make ultimate decisions, a judge or a doctor, a CEO, or governor, or on a smaller scale a juror or even a parent. It is about having authority associated with a position. It is a call to responsibility and it represents deserving the title and position of one's station in life. This is the sign of the natural -born leader, and the sign of someone who does what needs to be done.

Keywords

- Leadership

- Entitlement

- Power

- Authority

- Decisiveness

- Fire

- Action

- Elevated station

- The professions

- High expectations

- Ruthlessness

- Necessary actions

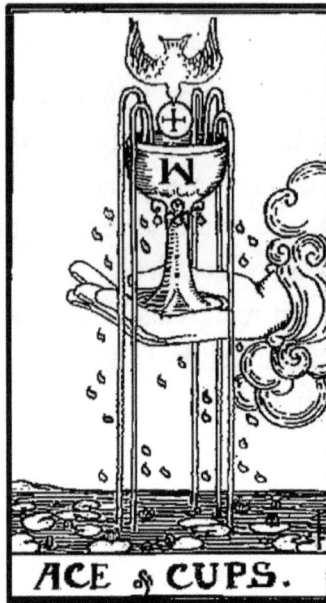

ACE ᴏꜰ CUPS.

Ace of Cups

Description

Here we see a large chalice being offered by the hand of the Divine. The chalice represents the mind, because it contains water, which is symbolic of emotions and spirituality. There is a dove descending into it with a communion wafer in its beak. This represents spiritual incarnation into the physical world. Water is streaming out of the cup into a large pond. This indicates the connection of our mind and spirit with the greater mind and spirit of the Divine. In the water there are lily pads and lotus blossoms. Lotus has always represented enlightenment. There is an upside down M on the cup, or is it a W? No one really knows for sure. It is the opinion of this writer that it represents both. One is the mirror image of the other and this corresponds to the mind's mirrored existence in both the astral and the physical realms simultaneously.

Interpretation

When this card is present in a reading, it often indicates good emotions. It can mean bliss or happiness. It can represent love and romance. It can negatively represent emotional difficulties or mental instability, but in general it's considered a positive card. Certainly, it stands for enlightenment and the spiritual concept of incarnation of the spirit into the physical world.

Keywords

- Enlightenment

- Incarnation

- Reincarnation

- Mind

- Emotions

- Happiness

- Emotional crisis

- Positive feelings

- Intuition

- Empathy

2 of Cups

Description

Here we see two figures, a man and a woman, and they are holding cups out to each other. There are hills of green in the background, representing life and fertility, as well as a house that indicates a soul. The caduceus of Hermes is between them but it is amplified by the lion's head instead of just the wings. The caduceus itself represents the planet mercury, which implies communication. The lion's head represents strength and power. With this the figure between them, it represents the strength and power of communication between the two parties.

Interpretation

One of the most popular interpretations of this card is that of soul mates or marriage. But this card can mean many other things as well. It can represent good partnerships, empathetic communications and a meeting of the minds. It represents diplomacy and agreement. It can also represent a strong friendship that is not necessarily romantic.

Keywords

- Love affair
- Soul mates
- Positive understandings
- Communications
- Diplomacy
- Meeting of the minds
- Marriage
- Dating
- Understandings
- Acceptance

3 of Cups

Description

We see in this card three women raising their cups in celebration. On the ground is an abundance of fruit representing abundance itself as well as health and fertility, and each woman has a wreath of laurel around her head, a sign of accomplishment and victory. Remember also that this is a "cup" card, and that there are other cards of celebration in the tarot, but this one is concerned with a cup; that is the emotions and spirituality. So this celebration can be seen as a form of spiritual success as well as any other kind of victory or celebration.

Interpretation

The 3 of Cups represents victory in all its forms. It's a very fortunate card to show up in any reading. It is positive and generally considered good luck. It can represent finding the right answer. It can represent celebration and a reason to celebrate. It represents winning and triumph. It is especially relevant in any kind of medical treatment, business deal, or legal matter. It can also mean a desired pregnancy.

Keywords

- Winning

- Decision in your favor

- Victory

- Spiritual ecstasy

- Triumph

- Success

- Desired Pregnancy

- Fertility

4 of Cups

Description

We see a solitary figure sitting under a tree. His arms are crossed, and he seems oblivious to the cup being handed to him by the Divine. In front of him are three other cups he has no desire for. He is dissatisfied and discontent. He is inwardly focused and emotionally withdrawn. Keep in mind that he is sitting on very fertile grass, and the tree he leans against is very green and alive. This indicates that he is ignoring the living world around him. Life is passing him by.

Interpretation

This card primarily represents an inward focus. It is generally a negative card, but it doesn't have to be depending on the context where it is found. It represents emotional withdrawal, and a discontentment with that which has been offered. This could certainly be interpreted as a sense of entitlement. It could also represent any kind of withdraw from life such as might be the case with depression or other mental ailments. On a positive note, the card can be interpreted as the Divine finally offering what is needed when nothing else has worked thus far. In that sense it can be seen as a solution.

Keywords

- Withdrawal

- Emotional unavailability

- Discontentedness

- Depression

- Apathy

- Wasting time

- The right stuff

- A Divine solution

5 of Cups

Description

In this card, a figure in a black cloak is staring down at the ground with his face hidden to us. He represents regret and despondency. Several emotional ventures have failed. He contemplates what it's all worth. There are five cups, but three of them are tipped over and spilled on the ground. These are failures and useless activities and investments. There are two left standing, but the figure has given up on them and turned his back to them. They are missed opportunities, for love or anything else. There is a stream flowing past and in the distance it is crossed by a stone bridge. This is symbolic of water under the bridge, wasted time and loss. There is a dark castle structure standing off on a hill, so even from a spiritual perspective we see this as a dark time in a person's soul.

Interpretation

This is a dark night of the soul. It represents missed opportunities and the loss of investment, especially emotional investments. It could mean failed marriages or relationships. It could mean the loss of connection with children or family members. It stands for existential angst and the contemplation of one's purpose in life. It can also represent giving up or a refusal to risk further investment. This is generally not a positive card, but it could be if indicates that a person would be better off giving something up.

Keywords

- Giving up

- Missed opportunities

- Loss

- Divorce

- Strained relationships

- Regret

- Despondency

- Falling out of love

- Lost friendships

6 of Cups

Description

This card is a difficult card for most people to understand. It has a lot of symbolism in it and opinions differ as to its core meaning. But certainly we see an older person is giving a younger person a cup with a flower in it. The cup with a flower represents blooming emotional contentment or spiritual enlightenment. It could also represent a gift of any kind. There are four cups in the foreground that are identical to the one in the older person's hands. This tells us that the recipient has been given this gift before. Since it is the older giving to the younger, we can assume these cups are elements of wisdom and experience of some sort. In addition, there is one cup left up on a pedestal, which indicates that there are more things to come. In the background is a castle, so we see that this has to do with the soul, and in fact, the cups seem to come from the bounty of the castle itself, indicating that the older person may well represent a previous lifetime and the younger would then be the current incarnation.

Interpretation

This card can mean generosity of any kind. It can mean giving a gift or receiving a gift. It can also represent the passing on of wisdom from the old to the young or from a previous lifetime to a current incarnation. Thus it could represent getting in touch with past lives. On a simpler level, it could mean a boy asking a girl on a date, because it seems to be a male giving a flower to a female who is looking up at him adoringly. For that matter it could mean simply giving the gift of love.

Keywords

- Proposal

- Courting

- Reincarnation

- Wisdom

- Giving gifts

- Receiving a gift

- Emotional healing

- Spiritual gifts

7 of Cups

Description

This is a complex card with a multitude of images. We see a man beholding seven cups in the clouds. The clouds represent a Divine presentation, so this is a vision the figure is having, and apparently he is being given a choice. One cup has a tower, indicating the pursuit of territory; another has jewels and chains indicating material wealth; another has wreath indicating achievement and superiority; another has a dragon representing intelligence and passion; another has a female head, indicating companionship or love, and another has a serpent, indicating vice and perhaps a temptation toward self-destruction. In the very middle is a hooded figure that is radiating light. This represents the occult mysteries.

Interpretation

When this card appears in a reading, on the most basic level, it represents having a choice to make. It can also represent the many paths a person might take in life or the confusion over which way to go. It can represent the ability to pick and choose. It can also represent the incarnations of a person, each one focusing on a different aspect of life overall. It can also represent wishful thinking or lacking focus, or even over-indulgence or partying too much.

Keywords

- Choices
- Decisions
- Paths
- Career choice
- Vocation
- Partying
- Over-indulgence
- Reincarnations
- Wishful thinking

8 of Cups

Description

Here we see that it's dark, and the moon is sad and looking down upon the nighttime landscape. This tells us that the setting is a depressive one. A figure is walking away from eight cups. He has turned his back on them and is heading off into the night. He walks beside a large river (indicating an emotional disposition). In the background are mountains indicating difficult times.

Interpretation

This is generally not considered a happy card. It tells us that depression and despondency are upon us. We have turned our back on the things that could bring us happiness. On a more basic level, this card represents simply walking away from something, or giving up. It can also mean the long road to recovery, especially in regard to addictions. Thus it can also represent the need for one to lay down old habits and walk away from bad elements in one's life. It can also mean starting off on a difficult or unwanted journey.

Keywords

- Giving up

- Depression

- Walking away

- Rehabilitation

- Addictions

- Leaving things behind

- Difficult journeys

- Fed up

9 of Cups

Description

In this card, we see a well-fed, satisfied figure sitting in front of a table where nine cups are placed like trophies. Obviously the figure is happy, and with his arms crossed, we get a sense of a certain satisfaction. This indicates emotional contentment. Even more the cups on display show that not only has the man achieved what he wants, but he shows it.

Interpretation

On a basic level, this card represents happiness. It represents getting what we want out of life. It represents contentment. It can also represent smugness or arrogance, and it can even represent obesity or having too much of a good thing. But in general, this card is a very positive card representing good fortune. It can also represent getting what one has sought after, thus it can stand for finding something that is lost.

Keywords

- Happiness

- Contentment

- Finding something

- Arrogance

- Smugness

- Over-indulgence

- Overweight

- Feeling good

10 of Cups

Description

In this card, we see a man and a woman standing underneath a rainbow that contains the ten cups. In the foreground children are playing, presumably their children. The sky is blue; the grass is lush; a stream runs past them, and in the distance is a nice house with a red roof. There's not much else going on, but this card has deep spiritual and practical significance. What we are looking at in this image is the astral plane itself. After death, when a person loses the blinders of the physical world, the astral plane reappears, and that's what this card is essentially showing.

Interpretation

First off, this card represents happiness or even bliss. It represents having everything a person could ever want. It represents the best of days and good times ahead. It represents the end of incarnations, and in that sense it represents heaven or nirvana. Certainly, it represents the kingdoms we build on the astral plane, but it can also represent a happy home life or a successful marriage. And since it is a cup card, it could also represent positive emotions or mental health.

Keywords

- Astral plane

- Happiness

- Bliss

- Mental health

- Happy home

- Good marriage

- Contentment

- Making it

- End of reincarnation

PAGE of CUPS.

Page of Cups

Description

Here we see a young man holding a cup with a fish coming out of it. His tunic has flowers on it, and he's wearing a blue headdress, this symbolizes spiritual wisdom. The fish is symbolic of the immature human soul. In this case, we see the deep spiritual elements of this card. It represents salvation, whatever that means to the querent, and redemption. In the background is a great rolling sea, indicative of the Divine.

Interpretation

One could see this card as indicating redemption, forgiveness, a peace offering, a second chance. It can have a more mundane meaning as well, and often does. It can mean a proposal, the meeting of a new romance, or the indication of a newborn child or pregnancy.

Keywords

- Salvation
- Forgiveness
- Peace
- Pregnancy
- New Romance
- A proposal
- A new soul
- A second chance

KNIGHT of CUPS.

Knight of Cups

Description

In this card, we see a knight wearing expensive cloth-ing and armor. A knight is almost always a messenger of some kind, and the horse represents a message coming toward us, or traveling to us. In his hand, he has a cup, and he's holding it out to the querent. His helmet has wings on it, and this symbolizes Mercury or more specifically, thinking and communication. There is a river in front of him pouring through a barren environment. This indicates emotions and creativity in a world where there is very lit-tle of that.

Interpretation

This card represents an awakening or an understanding that is unfolding or coming into ones awareness. It can represent increased knowledge from school, or an important message being delivered or coming to the querent. It can mean good communications and speaking that goes straight to the emotions. It can represent the idea for a novel or a work of art.

Keywords

- Inspiration

- Good communication

- A message

- Enlightenment

- Increased understanding

- Learning

- A proposal

- Creativity

- A novel idea

QUEEN of CUPS.

Queen of Cups

Description

This is a complex card; it has many symbolic elements associated with it. Notice we have a queen figure sitting on her throne. As a queen we see her as an elevated figure or someone of high evolution and refinement. Her throne sets on a small island of land in the middle of water. The body of water represents the Divine Mind, and her throne represents the seat of power and status. It has three cherub angels carved into it representing a throne of the angelic or heavenly realms. The cup she holds is different than any other cup in this suit. It is a closed container indicating hidden contents. She gazes upon it as if contemplating its interior. This is a symbol of occult knowledge and esoteric spirituality.

Interpretation

This cup stands for evolution through occult studies. It signifies a Divine status. It is the symbolism of Scorpio in astrology, and perhaps the 12th astrological house. It represents deep thought and paranormal divination. It represents witchcraft, and all forms of spiritual development. It represents a venture into the taboo, and an impending spiritual transformation.

Keywords

- Spiritual transformation

- Occult studies

- Taboo things

- Hidden mysteries

- Witchcraft

- Divination

- 12th house

- Scorpio

- Searching for wisdom

KING of CUPS.

King of Cups

Description

This is an incredibly powerful card. Here we see the final representation of all that the suit of cups represents. A king figure sits on a throne in the middle of a roaring ocean. This symbolizes a torrent of emotions, but the king is calm and sits as a master of the water. He holds a cup in his right hand and a scepter in his left hand. He is staring off into infinity, representing one who beholds the astral plane. He is calm because he sees beyond. He is dressed full royal regalia which further indicate his authority over the mind and emotions.

Interpretation

This card represents mental control, and calm. It can mean leadership in adversity or chaos. It can also mean rulership over emotions or supreme spiritual advancement. More mundanely, he represents a man who is even-tempered and can give emotionally, empathetically, and be caring as well as dominant. This would be a positive card in any reading and can even signify wealth associated with a controlled life.

Keywords

- A controlled life
- Mind over emotion
- Control of mind
- Spiritual advancement
- Empathy
- Wealth
- Even-temperedness
- Dominance through calm
- Calm
- Leadership in chaos

ACE of SWORDS.

Ace of Swords

Description

This card is the primary signifier of the suit of swords. Here we see the Divine reaching out from a cloud to hand us a sword that impales a crown. Thus, we see this as a gift from heaven. The crown symbolizes the rulership that comes to those who possess the sword. The vast barren landscape of the world serves as the background and symbolizes the cold nature of the uncompromising logical intellect. Fundamentally, this card is symbolic of the power of truth, truth in all its forms.

Interpretation

This card means knowledge. It means truth. It means intellect and psychic potential. All the manners of finding the truth are represented here: research, observation, psychism, divination, education, and memorization. It represents deep insight and understanding. It means power through knowledge, or a message from the Divine.

Keywords

- Knowledge
- Truth
- Divination
- Education
- Power
- Mind
- Intellect
- IQ
- Prophecy
- Message from the Divine

2 of Swords

Description

Here we see a female figure sitting with a blindfold on. This symbolizes A state of unknowing. She holds in her hands two swords pointing in opposite directions. This is symbolic of a dichotomy. And in the background is a large body of water, symbolizing the spirit of the Divine Mind. We get an impression of having two paths we can go on, and the truth of which is the right path is hidden from us.

Interpretation

The main interpretation of this card is the unknown. It means going into an uncertain circumstance. It means not knowing which the best path to take. It can also mean an argument where both sides have an equal validity. It can represent ignorance in all its forms, and it can represent the need for insight. .Since swords represent mind in all its forms, it can mean indecision, or a cloudy psychic impression.

Keywords

- Unknowing

- Ignorance

- Indecisiveness

- Opposing paths

- Choices

- Lies

- Deception

- Illusion

- Camouflage

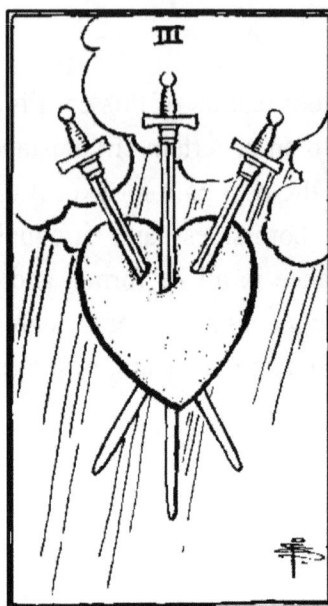

3 of Swords

Description

In this card, we see a heart skewered by three swords. This symbolizes a knowledge that hurts us to the core. There are storm clouds in the background, symbolizing upset and even and danger. It is raining, and this symbolizes tears associated with hard truths. This card is not usually considered a positive card, but as is the case with all such cards, it depends on the context of the query to which it pertains.

Interpretation

Bad news. A break up. A divorce. A truth that hurts. Deep personal insight that we don't want to face. For that same reason, the card also is indicative of psychotherapy. It can also have very practical meanings: a heart attack or coronary disease, unhealthy habits, or even death. It can mean the death of emotions that often comes with being overly academic. And it can represent a hardening of the heart brought on by bad experiences.

Keywords

- Heartache

- Heart disease

- Cynicism

- A break up

- A painful truth

- Psychotherapy

- Death

- Difficult Realization

4 of Swords

Description

In this card, we see a figure lying in repose. Some people think he is dead but that's not the case. He is at rest. His hands are in the position of prayer indicating deep meditation and communication with the divine. He is in a church, which symbolizes the house of the Divine, so this is a card that can also indicate travel to the astral realm. The three swords suspended above him indicate wisdom that is pouring in, and the single sword beneath him represents his rest being built on a foundation of wisdom and knowledge.

Interpretation

This card does not represent death, but it can represent a funeral, on a basal level. It represents comfort in knowing the truth. It represents Divine inspiration and even the reception of prophetic knowledge. It can simply mean a rest. And it can simply mean learning, or completing a course of study.

Keywords

- Rest

- Completion

- Graduation

- Prophetic insight

- Meditation

- Communion with the Divine

- Astral travel

- Esoteric knowledge

- Occult wisdom

- A funeral

5 of Swords

Description

Here we see a figure holding three swords. He has a knowing grin on his face as he watches two other figures walk away, apparently beaten or defeated. They have left their swords behind lying on the ground for the main figure to pick up if he chooses. There is a stormy sky and a large body of water which both represent stormy emotions, or if not that, then the great mind of the Divine.

Interpretation

This card is the card of discord and argument. It implies the querent will either win an argument or be defeated in an argument. It can also represent any kind of battle or competition where the victor has won through superior intellect or spiritual understanding. It can mean simpler things like scoring well on a test, being first in the class, or finally figuring out a problem. Depending on its context, it can also mean walking away from a useless fight or avoiding conflict.

Keywords

- Conflict

- Competition

- Fighting

- Superior intellect

- Winning

- Arguments

- Being first

6 of Swords

Description

We see in this card a figure pushing a boat along in the water. He symbolizes the circumstance that has brought about the change or the movement. On one side of the boat, the water is rough, on the other, the water is calm. Thus, we see the symbol of a conflicted mind. In the boat is a woman bundled up and hunched over and a small child sits beside her. This is symbolic of the whole of a life from child to adult. Therefore, the card can be seen as a life's journey. The swords in the boat represent the lessons we have learned along the way.

Interpretation

This card can mean many different things, and what it means depends substantially on the question that has been asked in the reading. For instance, it can represent a divorce, but not in a question that has nothing to do with marriage. It most often means taking a journey or a trip, traveling somewhere, or going through an experience. Some see it as a negative card, but it is really quite neutral. It can represent depression, or it can represent changing one's mind. It could even mean child custody.

Keywords

- Travel
- A trip
- Changing one's mind
- Divorce or separation
- Moving
- A conflicted mind
- Circumstances that push us
- A single mother or father
- Child custody

7 of Swords

Description

With this card, we see a figure sneaking off with five of the swords out of seven. There is an encampment in the background and the figure seems very satisfied with getting away. Symbolically, this card represents the upper class of the mentally superior and spiritually evolved. It can be interpreted many ways as described in the interpretation, but one has to keep in mind that this is a sword card, not a pentacle card. Therefore, it's basic symbology is not of one getting away with material goods, but rather getting away because of the mental and psychic gifts it has taken for its own.

Interpretation

This card represents getting away with it. It represents stealing and can mean sneaky, underhanded dealings. It can mean being a snake rather than a dove (from the saying of Christ that one should be as wise as a serpent and innocent as a dove). It can represent treachery, deceptiveness, cheating, and dishonor. But it can also represent prowess, and mental or psychic advantage.

Keywords

- Stealing

- Sneaky

- Advantage

- Prowess

- Having the edge

- Getting away with it

- Cheating

- Treachery

8 of Swords

Description

Here a woman stands bound and blindfolded. This symbolizes restrictions due to ignorance. She is surrounded by eight swords stuck in the ground and inaccessible to her. This means that for her condition, she is unable to gain the greater understanding needed for her soul, which is symbolized by an elevated castle in the background. Notice that she is standing in a swampy area, part land, part water. This symbolizes the cares of the world impinging on the wisdom of the spiritual realm.

Interpretation

This card can be seen as ignorance. It can mean restrictions of all kinds, but it can certainly mean restrictions that come from limited understanding. It can represent the unknown, and being trapped or persecuted. It represents a need for guidance, and possibly rescue.

Keywords

- Bondage

- Restraint

- Ignorance

- The unknown

- Limitations

- Spiritual stagnation

- Cares of the world

9 of Swords

Description

In this card, a figure is sitting up in bed at night. The figure has his face buried in his hands indicating regret. Nine swords hang over the bed, each one representing a reason for despair. This is not typically a positive card, but it symbolizes mistakes that all human beings make. If one looks closely, they will see that blanket is inscribed with all the constellations of the zodiac. This indicates all the fatalistic forces acting on a life, and we are shown that it is quite natural for people to generate regrets. A deep symbolism of this card is the fact that with great wisdom (the nine swords) comes great pain. And we are reminded that knowing the truth is not always a pleasant thing.

Interpretation

The card typically indicates remorse for the things we do wrong, or guilt, or regret over a bad decision. Thus, on a limited level, it can mean that a course of action will be regretted. It can also mean grief and despair. It is typically a card that gives us insight into a negative situation or warns us not to take a certain course of action. This card represents the dark night of the soul. The swords can either mean multiple worries, or the wisdom that is born of pain.

Keywords

- Regret

- Remorse

- Guilt

- Sadness

- Despair

- The pain of wisdom

- Worry

- Anxiety

- Fretting

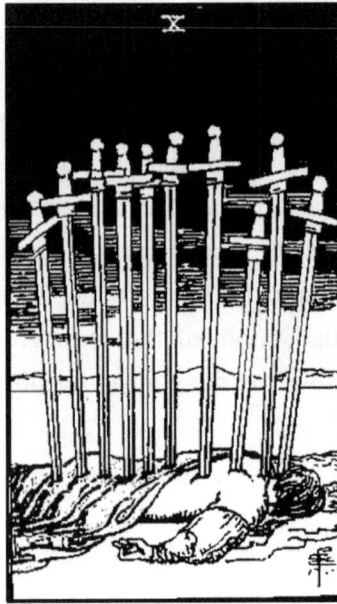

10 of Swords

Description

Here we see a figure lying on the ground. The background is night, and the landscape is unremarkable. What is remarkable is he has ten swords sticking out of his back. And he is, quite obviously dead. The orange robe that covers him mixes with the blood that is flowing underneath him. This is not a good-luck card. This card doesn't have a positive message. It is often a card that brings insight into a situation or a warning. However, depending on the context, it could be positive, especially if it refers to an enemy. But keep in mind that these are swords, so there is the deeper symbolism of dangerous thoughts or damaging ideas that a person might hold.

Interpretation

This card represents being mortally wounded. It signifies something bad is going to happen or has happened. It speaks to someone doing damage behind your back, or things that are out to hurt you. It can mean sacrifice and it can certainly mean death. Often this is seen as a card more indicative of physical death than even the Death card in the Major Arcana; therefore, it can certainly indicate murder or foul play. If there's no context for physical harm or death, it can certainly indicate a wrong idea, or dangerous way of thinking.

Keywords

• Death

• Bad luck

• A damaging course of action

• Dangerous thinking

• Destruction

• Bad health

• Murder

• Killing

PAGE of SWORDS.

Page of Swords

Description

With this card, we see a figure, a male (though in some decks this is a woman and is called the Princess of Swords), the wind is blowing, indicating the power of the Divine, also apparent by the billowing clouds in the sky. He is holding a single sword and facing into the wind. Thus we get our first hint that this lower royal figure is facing the power of God with the power of his mind, both analytical and psychic.

Interpretation

Often this card is interpreted as enthusiasm, the inspiration of an idea, the use of the mind to solve problems. To analyze, and to use one's psychic energies which are also part of the mind. The mind is, after all, both physically analytical and spiritually psychic. Both constitute mind. It can represent a teacher, or learning. It can represent the need to study, or it can represent thinking something through carefully, or the inspiration of an invention.

Keywords

- Inspiration
- Learning
- Teaching
- A new idea
- Revelation
- Examining beliefs
- Thinking something through
- Inventing

KNIGHT of SWORDS .

Knight of Swords

Description

Here we see a night on a horse. He is charging through a violent wind storm with his sword raised in attack posture. The horse is strained and the rider himself looks angry and aggressive. Thus, because this is a sword card, we know that this is the power of fundamentalistic thought. It is not rational, but rather intolerant and close-minded. We see discord and argument and a war of words.

Interpretation

This card can mean arguing, dogmatic beliefs, causes. It can also mean speaking with authority and confidence, expressing one's ideas with vigor, and maybe even violence. This is fundamentalism, and bigotry. But it is also the power of a clever argument, or a winning speech. A dominance in the courtroom, but it can also be direct and blunt, even rude. Simplistically interpreted, it could also indicate an urgent message.

Keywords

- Passionate expression

- Fundamentalism

- Directness

- Rudeness

- Vigor

- Cleverness

- Public speaking

- Winning dialog

- Opinionated

- Urgent message

QUEEN of SWORDS.

Queen of Swords

Description

In this card a queen is sitting on her throne, representing independence and dignity. It is a spring atmosphere indicating the birth of something new. Also the robe she wears has a springtime cloud pattern on it. In one hand she holds a sword, the symbol of mind, on her throne are engraved butterflies, and also his crown is rounded with butterflies. These are the symbol of transformation. Thus the primary symbolism of this card is one of transformation through mind, or transformation of mind.

Interpretation

The important interpretation of this card is one of transformation--mental transformation, especially, but any transformation is indicated. It represents the changing of one's mind based on new facts. It represents becoming something greater than you are. It represents a fool transforming into a wise person. It is the birth of a new mind, and in a concrete sense it represents a birth or pregnancy.

Keywords

- Transformation
- A change of mind
- New facts
- Evolution
- Modification
- Changes
- A new idea
- A pregnancy
- A new mind

King of Swords

Description

In this card we see the paragon of the sword. A king sits on his throne--this is the ultimate in authority. He holds a sword in his hand and his throne is engraved with butterflies, the symbol of transformation. In the background, we see a clear summer sky with clouds drifting by. This represents peace in the kingdom of the Divine. Thus, the ultimate symbolism of this card is one of intellectual and psychic superiority. This is a leader in all aspects of the mind and spirit. In many respects this is the image of God.

Interpretation

The King of Swords represents superior intellect. It could be a college professor or a leader in anything that requires mental activity such as a doctor, lawyer, scientist, or engineer. It represents institutions of higher learning as well as the educated class within society. More simply, it can mean being right. It can mean having authority via being smarter. It can represent a high IQ. But the mind includes the psychic potential as well. In that context, this card represents the pinnacle of psychic ability.

Keywords

- Mental authority

- Intelligence

- Being right

- The professions

- Psychic authority

- Education

- Teacher

- God

- Kingdom of the Divine

- Intellectual performance

Ace of Pentacles

Description

Like all the ace cards, we see a Divine hand holding out the object of the suit. In this case, it is a single pentacle. Notice in the background there is a fertile garden. On a spiritual level, this represents the Garden of Eden, or the ideal habitation for human beings. Pentacles, in general, represent material wealth, and in this card we see the material gain that comes to us as a gift from the Divine. It is the pinnacle of pentacles, if you will, showing the ultimate in wealth and comfortable living.

Interpretation

This card is generally considered a good luck card. In whatever context it is found, it means prosperity. This prosperity can be financial or any other form of prosperity --even spiritual, psychical, or physical. It means good things are coming. It means money is coming your way. It means comfortable living and success. It can also indicate first place or winning. It can mean having a wealth of something, abundant living, or an increase, or growth.

Keywords

- Winning

- Prosperity

- Abundance

- Growth

- Financial gain

- Finances

- Good luck

- Comfort

- Divine gifts

- Fertility

- A better life

2 of Pentacles

Description

This is a rather strange card. In it we see a juggler juggling two pentacles. They are connected by a band in the shape of the symbol for infinity; so on a deep symbolic level, this card represents the constant interplay between the spiritual life and the physical life, to include reincarnations. In the background, is the ocean, and it has great swells that the ships are attempting to sail. The ocean represents the power of God, and the ships represent the lives we live in service of the Divine. These are the deep meanings of this card. The interpretation in practice, however, is somewhat more mundane.

Interpretation

This card means juggling cares. It means a chaotic time or life. It means having conflicting issues. It also derives symbolism from the astrological sign of Libra, thus it represents finding balance, equity or justice. It represents the need to weigh options. It can represent business decisions or the need for decisions in any part of life. Because of the ocean symbolism, it can also mean finding one's purpose in life.

Keywords

- Decisions

- Balance

- Justice

- Conflict

- Chaos

- Busy

- Reincarnations

- Divine purpose

3 of Pentacles

Description

This fascinating card shows an artesian at work on a cathedral. This indicates the work we do on our soul in each incarnation. An architect and a friar stand with him and are discussing issues associated with the building. The friar represents a spirit guide, and the architect represents the Divine. Thus we see that it's a team effort to construct a valuable life. There are three pentacles carved into the arch of the doorway. This represents the wealth of wisdom that comes from several incarnations.

Interpretation

This card can mean deep spiritual things as well as mundane things. It stands for working on our spiritual selves. It can represent the input we receive from spirit guides. It represents a Divine plan for our lives. On a mundane level, it represents a job well done, teamwork, consultation, a meeting (especially related to work). It represents collaboration, partnership, and the need for partners in generating wealth. It can also represent the real estate industry or construction. It can also represent any artistic endeavor.

Keywords

- Teamwork

- Divine plan

- Spirit guides

- Incarnations

- Soul work

- Artistic endeavors

- Collaboration

- Meetings

- Plans

4 of Pentacles

Description

Here we see a minor ruler of sorts standing on two pentacles. This represents a material foundation. He is wearing one in his crown; this represents the power of money, and he's holding on tightly to the other. This represents the control that comes through having great wealth. He is planted on a stone throne which indicates immovability. In the background is a city. Thus we see two elements clearly: rulership and control. The city adds a political dimension to this card.

Interpretation

This card means control. It means political office, and executive status. It represents the power of money, and it represents the desperate need to hold on to it. It can also mean miserliness, penny-pinching, and the need to watch what we spend. It can mean running for office or position, and it can mean financial security or insecurity depending on the context of the reading. It can also mean resistance to change and the desire to keep things just as they are.

Keywords

- Control
- Money power
- Political office
- Financial standing
- Penny-pinching
- Security
- Insecurity
- Status quo
- Resisting change

5 of Pentacles

Description

In this card we see a desperate scene of a woman wearing a thin shawl, and a crippled, injured man walking behind her on crutches. This is not considered a good-luck card. They are partially barefoot, and obviously it is snowing. They are walking by a church with a stained glass window, and in the design of that window is five pentacles. What is not immediately clear is whether or not they are walking *to* the church for help, or if they are walking by the church that won't let them in. Depending on the context in which the card is laid, it could mean either.

Interpretation

This card typically means a loss of material income. It can mean homelessness. It can represent a failed business or misfortune of any sort. It can represent the need for charity, or it can represent the absence of charity. It can also indicate religious problems if one finds their church is not of use to them, or that they are at odds with it. It can mean bankruptcy, either financially or spiritually. It can also represent poor health.

Keywords

- Bankruptcy

- Homelessness

- Financial loss

- Charity

- Spiritual deprivation

- Want

- Poor health

- Eviction

- Desperation

- A hard time

6 of Pentacles

Description

In this card we see a wealthy merchant giving alms to the poor people who are kneeled down at his feet. Above him are six pentacles. Six, in astrological terms, is the house associated with service, and so this card has service connotations associated with it. It also, of course, has a basis of financial abundance and thus it is seen as a fortunate card in most readings. But it depends on the context, because the querent could be either the rich merchant or the beggars. The scale in the merchant's hand is indicative of justice, and thus the card may have implications related to the law.

Interpretation

The 6 of Pentacles can mean abundance, enough to give to charity. It can mean needing charity, or it can mean mercy. It can mean justice or fair play, but it can also mean servitude and lower forms of employment. It can mean management, and accounting. It can also mean generosity and caring.

Keywords

- Charity
- Need
- Begging
- Abundance
- Management
- Being the Boss
- Accounting
- Law
- Wealth
- Caring
- Support

7 of Pentacles

Description

Here we see a man leaning on a gardening tool. He is looking at what appears to be a grape vine, but instead of grapes we see seven pentacles. A grape vine represents the support of the Divine in spiritual terms, thus the pentacles represent the fruits of the spirit or psychic gifts. The background of this card is fairly insignificant, thus it focuses our attention on the central image.

Interpretation

This card means tending to a good crop, in whatever context that is relevant. It means a fortunate investment. It can mean the fruits of one's labor. It can mean, mundanely, a good year in agriculture. It can also mean winning in any context. It can also have spiritual implications and indicate the flourishing of psychic talents or spiritual gifts. It can also mean evaluation of progress or status.

Keywords

- Fruits of labor

- Good investments

- Agriculture

- Psychic gifts

- Working the land

- Tending to one's money

- Working to attain

- A good harvest

- Reviewing results

- Evaluating progress

8 of Pentacles

Description

In this card, the figure is actually creating pentacles. His previous works hang on a wooden beam in front of him, and lying on the ground and leaning up against the workbench are his works in various stages of progress. Thus we see this card is about *creating* in all its forms. It's about labor and making something out of the material world in which one finds oneself. In that sense, it refers to the work we are incarnated in the world to carry out. The castle in the background indicates the soul, and thus we see a connection between the soul, the physical world, and the work we do.

Interpretation

This card can mean working hard. It can represent a job or career. It represents making a living. It can also mean working on our purpose in life. It stands for craftsmanship and technical expertise. It represents being able to make money from one's talents. In that sense, it can represent being an artist or a creative person of some sort.

Keywords

- Job

- Career

- Craftsmanship

- Making money

- Technical mastery

- Following a purpose

- Work

- Persistence

- Creativity

- Artistic expression

9 of Pentacles

Description

In this card we see a woman standing in a vineyard. The vineyard represents the fruits of the spirit of the Divine. She is holding a flacon, and it has a hood on, and she has a falconry glove on. This represents patience and control. In the background is a house, which indicates the soul. The vineyard is infused with the nine pentacles, and the woman is wearing a flowing gown with flowers on it. The flowers are curiously in the shape of the symbol of Venus. Therefore, this card is about fertility and the latent or pregnant spiritual gifts within a person.

Interpretation

This card has many meanings. On one level it indicates fertility or pregnancy. It can also mean control over natural forces. It can easily mean wealth from business or success, since the vineyard seems to be producing wealth. It can mean self-control, as the figure looks on but does not disturb the bird. It represents independence and even solitude, or perhaps being better off being alone.

Keywords

- Independence

- Pregnancy

- Self-control

- Control in any form

- Business success

- Latent psychic gifts

- A prosperous life

- A secret garden

- Better off alone

10 of Pentacles

Description

This is a rather complicated card with lots of imagery. In the foreground is an old man sitting down wearing a opulent robe and petting his dogs. In front of him are his adult children; one of them may be the spouse of his child. Behind them is their child, and in the background is a large castle structure. Thus this card is about inheritance and legacy, both the spiritual legacy we leave (the castle) and the legacy of wealth we leave behind.

Interpretation

This card can mean retirement, financial stability, conservatism, and inheritance. It can represent all manner of financial planning, and it represents a good life from sound investments. It can mean leaving a legacy. It can mean having it all, spiritually and materially. More simply, it is the card of welfare; that is seeing to the welfare of others and for the welfare of animals.

Keywords

- Inheritance
- Retirement
- Legacy
- Opulence
- Generational wealth
- Generations
- Child and Animal welfare
- Building a life
- Wills

PAGE of PENTACLES.

Page of Pentacles

Description

Here we see a young man standing in a fertile field holding a large pentacle in his hands and looking up to it with some kind of wonder. We can see that the sky is clear and bright, and thus we envision a dreamer. One who believes they will find something of value. In that way, the basic symbolism of this card is one of wishful fantasy or the hope of a new beginning. Since pages are often associated with new beginnings or new starts, clearly this card has a fundamental meaning of hope for the future.

Interpretation

this is the card for those thinking of starting a business. It could represent a lottery ticket, wishes, hopes for material gain, the desire to be of a better class or to move up the social ladder. It represents a fresh start; it can more mundanely represent finding money or finding something of value. It can also represent seeing the material rewards inherent in an idea. Or it can simply mean seeing or recognizing the value in something.

Keywords

- Hope for the future

- Business beginnings

- Wishing for rewards

- Starting out

- An entrepreneurial idea

- Recognizing value

- Moving up

- A valuable idea

KNIGHT of PENTACLES.

Knight of Pentacles

Description

With this card we see a well-armored knight holding out a pentacle. He is on a dark horse and is unmoving. Everything is in place, and even the background holds little surprises, but is instead a very mundane agricultural field of some sort. The horse is large, and steady, and can easily support a lot of weight. Thus the central symbolism of this card is one of security and conservatism. There are no chances being taken, and little excitement to be had.

Interpretation

This card is all about steady, planned, ventures. It's about saving money in a traditional way rather than investing. If it is investing, then it is blue chip stocks, solid business ventures. Being a knight, it means a message, in this case a message to be fiscally conservative, to be responsible, to be steady and steadfast, to not take chances. It calls us to pay attention to details, to make sure all things are in order. It represents commitment, and honor in our dealings.

Keywords

- Steady
- Conservative
- Committed
- Responsible
- Obsessive with details
- Saving money
- Frugalness
- Low risk
- Traditional
- Institutional

QUEEN of PENTACLES

Queen of Pentacles

Description

In this card a queen sits in full regalia upon her throne. The background is one of abundance and fertility. She holds in her lap a large pentacle, indicating a great value is in her possession. She is contemplating it and looking down on it with concern and caring. Thus, we see this card representing benevolence and nurturing. It is a royal card so it is powerful in its meaning, and its spiritual dimension is one of a spirit guide looking down toward her earthly charge. Mundanely, it can also indicate a woman who is doing well on her own, or it could represent a favorable pregnancy.

Interpretation

This card can mean many things. It can represent female independence, an inherited wealth left to a spouse, it can simply mean having royal dignity, or abundant material possessions. It implies generosity, and a caring attitude. It is symbolic of spirit guides or angels. It carries with it a meaning of Charity and concern

Keywords

- Generosity

- Kindness

- Caring

- Nurturing

- A spirit guide

- Concern

- Charity

- Bounty

- Fertility

- Felinity

- Pregnancy

King of Pentacles

Description

We see with the King of Pentacles a complex card with lots of symbolism. A king sits on a large throne, grapes and abundant vegetation surrounds the throne. This indicates wealth in all its forms and the means of gaining wealth in the material world. The king holds a pentacle in one hand and in the other holds a scepter. Thus, the card indicates power and financial authority. Images of a bull's head are on each corner of the throne, linking this card with the symbolism of Taurus in astrology. As such, it is the main symbol of material possessions and security in the physical realm. In the background is a massive castle structure, and this brings in a spiritual dimension to this card. It indicates a Divine right to wealth and power. It represents the idea of the establishment and the way the world works.

Interpretation

This card can mean a bank or financial institution. It means power and authority in the material world. It can certainly mean abundance, but it can also very mundanely mean a person's employer or someone else who holds the purse strings of wealth. It can represent a father, and it can represent stability, commitment, determination, and perseverance. Thus it represents success.

Keywords

- Success

- Institutional Wealth

- Banks

- Employer

- Commitment

- Determination

- Perseverance

- Taurus

- Material possessions

- Power

5

The Spread Ritual

In this chapter, we are going to begin the journey into the dark art of tarot. We've looked at the history of the cards, the way to choose a deck, and the meaning of each card in the deck. Now, we are headed into the magical ritual itself.

When tarot is used for entertainment only, the magical system involved in the sorcery of tarot can be ignored. In that case, one simply grabs a deck, shuffles it, and lays the cards out in a Celtic Cross spread (See page 196.), and then they apply the standard definitions and keywords to those cards.

That practice does in fact provide a reading for the querent, but a computer can also do that kind of reading, and in fact there are several tarot reading computer apps in existence; just Google them! The results, however, from such an entertainment approach are no better than chance in terms of accuracy. If one wants accuracy and insight, they have to treat tarot as the sorcery that it is.

I've included the Celtic Cross spread for those who wish to go no further into the dark art of tarot. On the opposite page, you'll find the way to lay it out. You can stop reading this book at that point and enjoy the entertainment aspects of tarot with friends and family, perhaps even with paying customers!

But if you choose to continue, we will examine the true ritual that produces real results. The information that follows is for the sorcerer only.

We will look at the sorcerer's three-card spread and the progression spread, and how to do them properly. we will look at the equipment one needs for their altar and how it is used; we will then look at the philosophy of darkness, and it may surprise you to find that it has nothing to do with evil, but is actually the opposite of evil.

Where you go with tarot from this point is up to you, but if you're ready to learn secrets of this dark art, then let's continue.

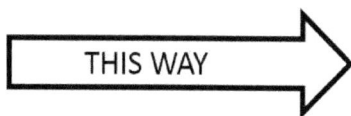

THIS WAY ⟹

3

1

10

2

6   5   9

4   8

7

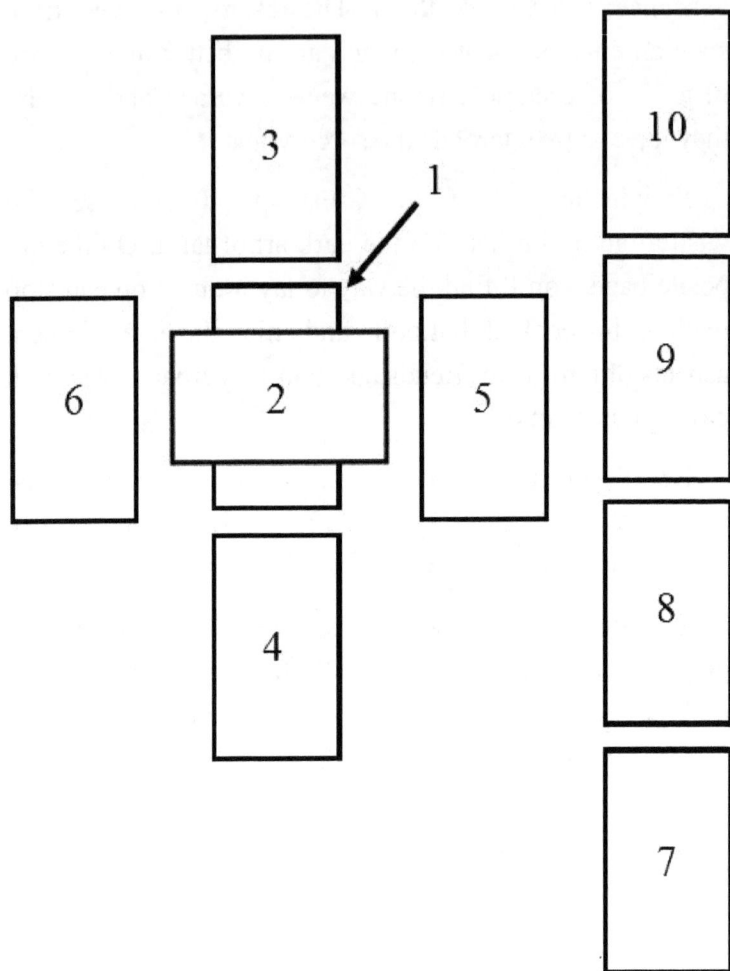

Celtic Cross Spread

Card 1: (Present) The present situation or the present state of the querent's mind.

Card 2: (Challenges) Restrictions and challenges crossing the querent's path. The problem the querent is facing.

Card 3: (Past) This represents the past or events that have led up to the present situation.

Card 4: (Future) This is the immediate future. It's not the end of the reading, but more like the next thing to happen in the situation.

Card 5: (Above) This is what the querent is aiming for, what their goal or aspiration ins for the situation.

Card 6: (Below) What is subconsciously driving the client.

Card 7: (Advice) Recommendations for the querent.

Card 8: (External) These are influences outside the querent's control that affect the situation.

Card 9: (Hopes and Fears) These are the hopes or the fears or both that the querent is feeling about the situation.

Card 10: (Outcome) This is how the situation will work out, if the querent understands the reading and follows the advice.

Now that you've examined the Celtic Cross, let's look at the sorcery of tarot.

There is a certain way to do this magical ritual, and if it is followed, the cards will become paranormally ordered so as to provide an answer to the question the querent has posed to the sorcerer. In order to get the most out of the ritual, however, one must first understand the six spiritual dynamics at work in this form of sorcery.

1. The Divine

2. The Question

3. The Perception

4. The Shuffle

5. The Cut

6. The Spread

The Divine

The sorcerer must believe the Divine will honor the reading he or she is trying to accomplish. This is a relationship of faith. The sorcerer believes this faith relationship works because of past experience. It has always worked for the sorcerer, and so they have every expectation that the Divine will honor all their spreads if they are repeated in the same manner, because the Divine always has. A secondary effect of this faith that many sorcerers report is that it produces a feeling closeness with the Divine.

This is where a point of contention can arise. Is a sorcerer required to believe in the existence of the Divine? Is this not a religious question and open to religious interpretation? The answer is yes and no.

Yes, the sorcerer must believe in the Divine. If they don't, then who do they think is ordering the cards?

But, no, there is no religious requirement. What the Divine is, how the Divine operates, these are questions each sorcerer answers according to their own religious inclinations.

Lots of different people practice tarot divination, and they are from a variety of religious backgrounds. Wiccans, Buddhists, Muslims, Christians, Jews, Sikhs, and Hindus, can all be found, especially online, practicing tarot, not to mention the more eclectic New Age practitioners and independent witches.

I have known tarotists from all these backgrounds. What they share is a belief that some greater mind within the universe is ordering the cards according to their request to know the answer to the querent's question.

The Question

If the spell of a tarot reading is going to work, the querent must be the one asking the question, and they must ask the right kind of question in the right way. The question must be their own, it must be specific, it must be important to them, and the answer must be otherwise unknowable to them. Let's look at each requirement more closely:

The question must be the querent's.

It would be totally inappropriate for a tarot reader to suggest a question to the querent. In fact, if they do, the spell simply won't work and the reading will be no greater than chance.

If you, as the reader, say to the querent, "Would you like to know if you're going to be rich in life?" and the querent shrugs their shoulders and says, "Sure, why not?" That's not a question that will work with a tarot reading. It is not the *querent's* question.

In such a case, the querent really isn't even a querent. The reader becomes the querent, but because the reader thinks the question is the querent's, because they don't realize they have switched rolls with the querent, it throws the intention of the spell into chaos.

Chaotic intention in any spellwork throws off or nullifies a spell. This is so in all forms of magic and especially so in the sorcery of tarot divination. Intention must be focused on the right target. The querent must be the one asking the question, and the reader must be the one performing the reading. Reverse the rolls, and the intention is no longer focused.

Granted, in private, a reader could do a reading all by themselves and ask, "Will that person be rich in life?" The spell would work in that case, because there is no chaos in the rolls of the spell. The reader is fully aware that they are also the querent and that the question is actually their own question. There's no role confusion, thus no chaotic intent, and therefore the divination spell can work.

The question must be specific.

You will frequently encounter querents who ask question like this: "I would like a reading on my finances and also if I'm going to be married and how many children I will have."

This is a completely inappropriate question for a tarot reading, at least for a single tarot reading. There are three questions being asked in one. It causes a *diffusion of intent* on the part of the sorcerer and the spell will be nullified as a result.

When the cards are dealt into a spread, they refer to a single question. If a querent asks multiple questions, they are trying to derive multiple meanings from a single card. It doesn't work. The sorcerer must insist that the querent choose which of the three elements of that question he or she would like a reading on the most. Otherwise a reading will result that is no greater than chance.

The question must matter.

A more common problem occurs, and it can be very subtle, but it is probably the number one most common reason a tarot reading fails. Sometimes a querent just doesn't care about the question they're asking. They just want to have some fun by getting a reading.

Tarot readers should realize that while they can charge for these readings and make money off these disingenuous customers, the readings themselves are actually worthless. It's this writer's opinion, therefore, that a sorcerer is ill-advised to do such readings. After all, the sorcerer has a relationship of faith with the Divine, and that relationship can only suffer if it is abused or taken in vain.

If a client is giggly, if they can't seem to think of a question to ask, if they seem skeptical or seem to be "testing the psychic," if they ask a ridiculous question, all of these are indicators that the query is not important to the querent. The sorcerer can put as much will and intent into the ritual for such questions, but it is unlikely the Divine will order the cards.

In fact, the Divine may allow evil influences to order the cards to match the disingenuous intent of the querent. In that case, you may find that you've given a seriously paranormal reading, but the querent has been sent away (unknown to you or them) with the worst possible advice. This can actually be quite dangerous, so the querent should be advised to ask a question that *seriously* matters to them.

The answer must be unknowable.

Tarot is magic. It produces a paranormal result in the form of foreknowledge we call divination. It makes the unknown known. This is the fundamental result of the spell. If a querent knows the answer already, or can easily know the answer, then to use spellwork to foresee the answer would again abuse the faith relationship the sorcerer has with the Divine.

For example, one could ask "Will my car be in the parking lot when I go out to look at it?" But, of course, all one has to do is get up and go look in the parking lot to find out. There is no need for paranormal divination in that question. The question is too petty and easily determined right here in the physical world, using one's physical senses, to invoke the Divine in such a vain reading. It would be spiritually insulting. The reading—at best—would result in no better than chance.

A common permutation of this is when a client asks a question that can only be determined by their free will. A young woman may ask, "Will I have children in the future?" This seems like a legitimate question, but it rests on the querent's free will. Assuming there's nothing obstetrically wrong with the woman, what she is asking is whether or not she will decide to get pregnant—but that's her choice. What she implies is that she has no choice, and that fate will automatically decide if she will have children. The universe simply doesn't work that way.

Fate operates on *impotent ignorance*. That is, it only works if the subject does not know the future or cannot control the future, or both. Free will is the opposite. It operates on *informed consent*. That is the subject knows what will or will not happen and chooses to go one way or the other.

One way we know what will happen is to decide to take action and *make* something happen. If a querent asks a question of the reader that the querent has free will to control, the result of the reading will be invalid.

If the reader says, "Yes, the cards say you will have children," the woman could say, "But I don't want children," and then she may take steps to avoid getting pregnant, thus making the reading wrong. Or she could say, "Good, I always wanted children," and the cards would only be stating her choice by chance, because if they had said she wouldn't, she could have used her free will to again make them wrong.

Later on, we will see how the principle of the unknowable answer is used to turn a bad reading into a warning for the querent. That is once the querent learns that a bad thing that will happen, they can use their free will to render the reading incorrect. This is perfectly legitimate and not a violation of the faith relationship the sorcerer has with the Divine. It's a legitimate tool given by the Divine in the sorcery of tarot.

Nevertheless, in order for a tarot reading to be accurate, the answer to the question must be unknowable by any other way. If it can be determined by the querent by physical means, then a tarot reading is inappropriate. If it can be answered by a free will choice, then a tarot reading is inappropriate.

The Perception

Assuming a question is appropriate for a tarot reading, then the sorcerer must perceive the question from the querent. This can be done in person; it can be done online; it can be done over the phone. The important thing is that the sorcerer internalizes the question from the querent so that it is in his or her mind. This mental adoption of the querent's question is what allows it to be telepathically transmitted to the Divine during the shuffling.

If the question is too vague, this principle of perception can be violated, thus rendering the reading ultimately in-accurate. If there is a language barrier, if the querent doesn't make sense (perhaps because they don't express themselves well in writing), or if the querent is intoxicated in some way, the perception of the question can be blocked. Make no mistake, the question must be clearly communicated to the sorcerer in order for the tarot ritual to work.

Because understand that what is really going on with a tarot reading is that the querent is abdicating to the sorcer-er the task of reading the tarot cards for themselves. The querent could do their own reading, if they knew how, but it is assumed they don't, so they are going to an expert who does. That expert, the sorcerer, must understand the question in order to communicate it to the Divine.

It's not enough to say, "God knows your heart." That may be true, and the Divine may choose to communicate with that individual in any number of ways, but we are

talking about tarot divination, and tarot divination is a ritual of spellwork performed by a sorcerer who knows how
to apply it.

Given that context, then the sorcerer must correctly
perceive the querent's question in order to serve as a
proxy for the client. They must ask for clarification if they
don't understand, and they must refuse the reading if they
can't get it.

The Shuffle

Shuffling the cards is one of the key concepts in tarot
divination. It is the shuffling that *orders* the cards. The
idea is that the sorcerer telepathically transmits the
querent's question to the Divine; The Divine, in turn, con-
trols the mind of the sorcerer such that the shuffling will
order the cards for the predetermined spread.

The shuffle has three components which will discuss in
turn: *the shuffle stop, communicating intent, determining
the spread*, and *cutting the deck*.

The Shuffle Stop

There is no set amount of time or manner in which cards
must be shuffled. In whatever way you know how to shuffle the cards, that will do. How long you shuffle the cards is
really up to you as well, but you should only shuffle the
cards until you feel an intuition that it is time to stop.

When you first get an inclination that it's time to stop
shuffling, do not shuffle the cards any further. If you keep

going, you will nullify the reading, and it will be off and inaccurate as a result. It will then be no more accurate than chance.

The ability to feel the intuition to stop shuffling is one of the primary skills of tarot divination. Normally, shuffling takes the better part of a minute, but how long you shuffle and when you stop is the primary telepathic communication you get from the Divine during a reading. So it's important to develop that sense of intuition. The more you do tarot readings, the more certain you will be of the appropriate shuffle-stop.

Just shuffle the cards and when you get a sense that you should stop—do not shuffle beyond that point.

Communicating Intent

While you are shuffling the cards, you must speak to the Divine in your mind and ask that he or she (depending on your conception of the Divine) order the cards for your querent's question. If a querent (Let's call her Ms. Jones.) were to ask me the following question: "Will my court case be settled in my favor?" This is how my own communication with the Divine would go:

Divine Creator, show me the answer to Ms. Jones question. Will the court case be settled in her favor? (I keep shuffling). Divine Creator, please give me the knowledge of this query. How will her case go?"

Then, if I felt the intuition, I would execute a shuffle-stop at that point.

If a card falls out while you are shuffling, there is no additional meaning. Just put the card back in the deck and keep shuffling. The card falling out, and your putting it back in the deck is all part of the supernatural way in which the Divine is ordering the cards.

Every movement you make while shuffling is actually the Divine using your body to order the cards. The same advice applies should you spill the cards all over the place on accident--the fact is it was no accident. Pick up the cards, put them back together, square the deck, and resume shuffling.

Try not to look at the cards while shuffling, and make sure they are all face-down before you begin. Shuffle them in such a way that you only see the backs of the cards. Seeing the images of the cards while you are shuffling them causes *impedance* in the telepathic transmission of the query between you and the Divine.

The Cut

When you have finished shuffling the cards, the last thing you do is *cut the deck*. This is how you put a brake on the Divine controlling your movements.

There is no irreverence in this, because it is part of the work you are doing in partnership with the Divine, but don't be surprised if you feel the loss of the connection.

You may feel a slight sense of emptiness when you stop communicating the query in order to cut the deck.

This is normal, because to be connected with the Divine is a fundamental desire of human beings. Don't worry about it; just let it motivate you to do more readings in the future so that you can feel that same connection again.

When you cut the deck, try to be as casual about it as you can. You cut the deck into three piles from left to right, and then you restack them from left to right. Then square the deck.

Do not try to make the stacks even. Do not try to do anything except drop some cards at random into three stacks. They will be uneven, maybe even dramatically so. It's important to let them be as they are.

The Tri-Stack Split

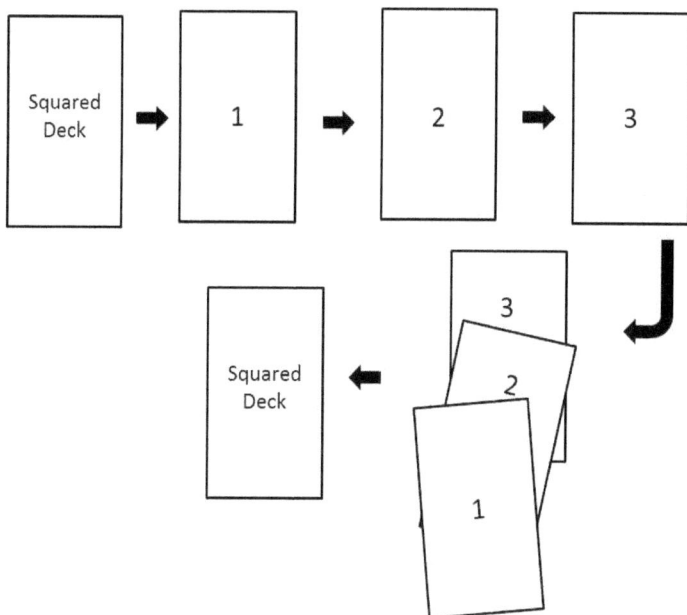

The Spread

At this point you have shuffled the cards and cut them. You are now holding the squared deck in your hand. The Divine has ordered the cards *based on the spread you intended to do from the beginning and the ritual* you performed in shuffling and cutting them. The spread, therefore, is the pattern of cards that lie on the table after you deal them from the deck.

Important!

You must **predetermine the spread** you will use before you begin your shuffle. For instance, if you change your mind in the middle of shuffling and decide you want to switch from a three-card spread to a progression spread, you must stop shuffling and start the ritual over. I recommend waiting an hour to let all psychic energies clear before starting over.

There are hundreds of different spreads one can do, lots and lots of specialized ways of laying the cards. But in truth they all boil down to two archetypal spreads: The *three-card spread*, and the *progression spread*.

The Celtic Cross, for instance, is an amplification of the three-card spread. Most multiple card spreads where the cards are dealt one at a time are some derivation of a progression spread. The sorcery of tarot, however, requires one to use these two archetypal spreads.

The three-card and progression spreads are the spreads the system of tarot was designed for. And while some may find this approach quite rigid, remember we are not dealing with entertainment or personal artistic expression; we are dealing with a form of magic that has specific and rigid ritual requirements that the Divine correspondingly honors with prophetic wisdom. It's assumed the reader wants accuracy in divination--not entertainment.

The Three Card Spread

The first thing you must understand about the three-card spread is that it ties in with astrology. Astrology is the non-psychic study of the position of planets and stars as they relate to events that occur on the earth.

Astrology describes fatalistic forces that act upon the physical world. It makes sense then that any symbolic system used to divine the future would have to have some relationship to astrology.

The mechanism that ties astrology to the three-card spread is not clearly understood, but it is known to work. I always use it, and I have produced truly supernatural readings as a result. The good news is you don't have to know a lot about astrology to make it work.

What you do have to know is the houses of the Zodiac. There are twelve of them, and each one deals with an aspect of life in the physical world. It's easy to understand.

On the next page is the house division of a chart wheel. A chart wheel represents the zodiac. Each house represents thirty degrees, and all twelve together make up the 360 degrees of the circle.

It's important to know the keywords for these houses, because when you deal cards for the three-card spread, you will deal out the card for the particular house that best represents the querent's question.

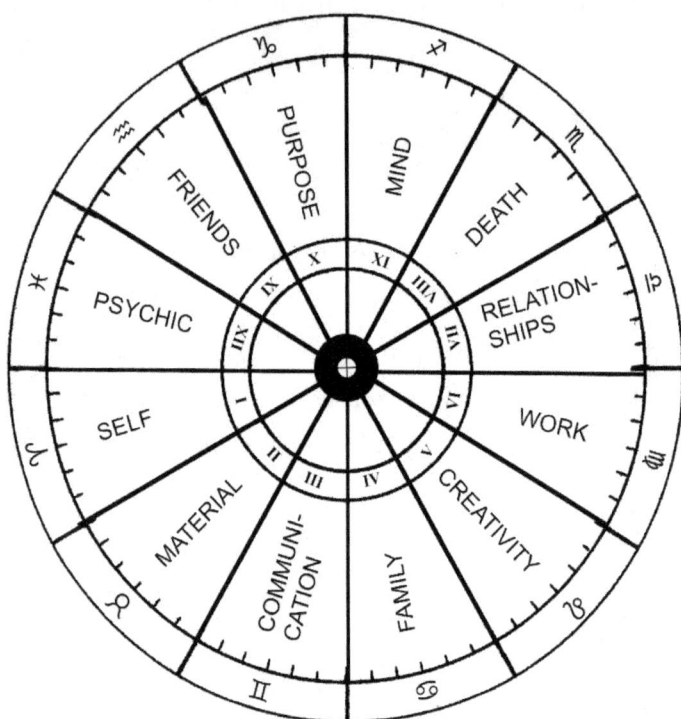

Houses of the Zodiac

For instance, let's say the querent has asked a question about their finances. As you can see the *second* astrological house deals with material things. Finances would naturally fit into that category; therefore, you would deal out the second card from every twelve cards until three cards are laid on the table.

An alternative way would be to deal the cards from the top of the deck and actually lay each card in order in the houses of the zodiac.

So, a card in 1, a card in 2, a card in 3, and so on until there was a card in each of the twelve houses. You would then repeat this this three times and pick up the stack of three cards from the second house.

The card on top would be the third card laid, so it would be the *future card*. The card in the middle would be the second card that was laid, and that would be the *present card*, and the first card that was laid in the second house would be the *past card*.

Most people, however, don't' have a big zodiac circle they can use to lay cards in. And it's not necessary. All you have to do is deal out the cards and count each card until you get to twelve. Just make sure you set card #2 to the side.

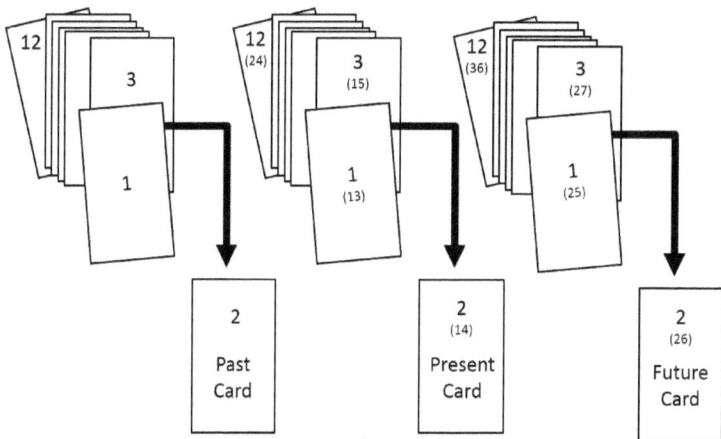

Dealing on the second house

So, you would start dealing: 1,2 (2 goes to the side as *the past card*),3,4,5,6,7,8,9,10,11,12. Now restart the count and deal 1,2 (2 goes to the side as the middle card, *the present card*),3,4,5,6,7,8,9,10,11,12. Restart the count: 1,2 (2 goes to the side as the third card, *the future card*). And that's it.

You don't even have to finish dealing out the last cards of the deck, because they aren't going to be used anyway.

You now have three cards laying face down on the table.

Always deal the cards face down. If you don't, it will distract you psychically. You want the first time you lay eyes on the cards to be all at once, and you only want to see the cards of that particular tarot spread, no others.

The rest of the cards you can collect up, square the deck, and set to the side. Your deal is done. The spread is laid. That's it. From this point forward you will go on to interpret the cards, but the ritual is finished.

Flip all three cards over at once. Turn all cards up. *Do not read reversed cards.* Reversed cards mean nothing. The cards were designed to be read right-side up.

I realize that some readers consider a different meaning for reversed cards, and there is some historical precedence for this, but there are no definitions or keywords specifically for reversed cards. A reversed card is considered to be a negation of the natural keywords associated with the upright card itself.

Ultimately, to read or not to read reversed cards is a denominational difference in the practice of tarot. All I can say is that *my* system, which is described in *this* book, has given me great results, and I believe it will for you, too. Therefore, I can't teach or write about any other way. The rule in my system, therefore, is not to read reversed cards.

That said, what you have laying in front of you is the message the Divine has given you regarding the querent's question. It is symbolized in the images of the cards.

Now, the *position* of each card has a special meaning. Consider the following:

The Past Card

This is the card on your left. It is the "past" card. It represents the circumstances, issues, or state of being that existed prior to the present moment. It shows what has led up to the present moment when the reading is being done. It provides background.

Quite often it provides insights into the motivations of the querent, but it also helps validate the reading. For instance, given the following query: *Will I get rich from my new business venture?* If the first card is the Page of Pentacles, it helps to validate the reading, because that card often represents an entrepreneur.

The odds of that card showing up in that position for that kind of question is highly unlikely. Yet if it shows up, even if it doesn't tell us much, because we already knew the querent was an entrepreneur starting a business, it does serve to *validate* the reading.

Sometimes a reading is called "spooky" when it is *highly validated*. That means that only a supernatural explanation for the cards that showed up in the spread explains the possibility of it, at least to any degree of common sense.

The Present Card

This is the middle card, and it is the present card. It shows the querent's current state of being. It may also show a decision that's under consideration or events going on in the querent's life.

It can provide insights from which you might advise the querent, and it also provides validation. Given the same question as above, "Will I get rich from my new business venture?" if the second card comes up, say the 5 of Pentacles, this would tell us that right now the client is in need of making some money.

And if that card actually showed up with that question, when the past card was the 4 of Pentacles, you would be dealing with a highly validated reading. So much so that unless someone saw it happen, they might not believe it did happen. You would be experiencing a miracle. Fortunately, using the system in this book, two-card validation happens all the time.

The Future Card

This card shows the future. It is the card to your right. It shows what will happen, or provides advice to follow, or shows the consequences of an action.

If the rest of the reading is validated to your satisfaction, you have every reason to believe the future card is actually telling you the future, as well, assuming it's interpreted correctly.

Let's say, given our querent's question, we get the Tower card in the third position. We can trust that a card that represents ruin is telling us that the particular business venture will lead to the querents ruin in some respect. Of course if it turns out to be the 4 of Wands, the card of celebrations and success, then the opposite would be true.

Past Card	Present Card	Future Card
• Past events • Background info • Validation	• Current situation • Current events • Decisions	• Future events • Consequences • Advice

Helpful Tips

The three-card spread works best if you keep in mind the following tips:

- Only read upright cards. Turn upside-down cards upright.

- Never deal or shuffle the cards face-up; always do so face-down, so you don't see any of the images beforehand.

- Turn all three cards over at the same time. Do not turn them over one at a time. This way the entire psychic picture hits you all at once and no stray thinking interferes with it.

- Do not re-deal if you don't like the cards you have. That renders the reading worthless. It removes the Divine control of the cards and returns them to a chance occurrence. The only exception would be if you made a mistake in the ritual, like you forgot to cut the deck, or you dropped the deck while you were dealing, or you miscounted the cards as they were coming off the deck, something like that.

- If you are doing a reading in person, never let the querent touch the deck. You are the sorcerer, you are doing the ritual. A priest wouldn't let someone reach in and get their own Host during mass; the same reasoning works for you. It's *your* ritual, with *your* cards, *your* manipulation of them, *your* energy, and *your* relationship of faith with the Divine. You are the only one qualified to perform the ritual.

The Progression Spread

There is another spread sorcerers use; it's called the progression spread, or simply *a progression*. It is essentially a bunch of single, present-card readings. It's used when you want to provide a message from the Divine Creator to the querent. In essence, it's used to conjure or channel the Divine, and it's very helpful in spiritual counseling.

The phenomena of validation and astrological coordination are not present, nor are they necessary. Here's how it works:

First you shuffle the cards as before, but this time you ask the question, and when you feel the psychic stop, you take the first card off the top of the deck and lay it down face up. That is the answer to that question.

You then repeat that process and explore the subject until you are psychically satisfied you have the complete message. This feeling would be equivalent to the afore-mentioned *psychic stop.*

It may be easier to understand with a script. Consider the following scenario; we will use the same question from the querent we used before, *Will I get rich from my new business venture?*

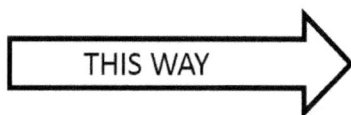

THIS WAY →

⇒ Shuffle the cards while thinking:

⇒ *Divine Creator, will this person be rich from their business venture?*

⇒ Feel the psychic stop and flip a card off the top of the deck; it is the 5 of Swords.

⇒ Interpreted answer: *She will have to be better than her competition.*

⇒ Again, shuffle the cards while thinking:

⇒ *What is the nature of her competition?*

⇒ Feel the psychic stop and flip the card off the top of the deck; this time it is the 2 of Pentacles.

⇒ Interpreted answer: *They are willing to gamble, to risk more.*

⇒ Again, shuffle the cards while thinking:

⇒ *What are the risks she must take?*

⇒ Flip the card off the top of the deck; it is The Fool

⇒ Interpreted answer: *She must be willing to venture into uncharted areas, new areas.*

⇒ Again, shuffle the cards while thinking:

⇒ *What would prevent her?*

⇒ Flip the card off the top of the deck; it is 8 of Swords.

⇒ Interpreted answer: *She is bound by her present circumstances; she must do what is required to break free.*

As you can see, the progression can go on for as long as you want it to. But there will come a point when you know you've answered the querent's question fully, and further interrogation of the Divine is not required.

Feeling the psychic stop while interrogating the deck and feeling it when the question is fully answered is the key to a good progression reading. You have to know when to stop shuffling, and when to stop the whole reading. That's the psychic talent of it, and it gets better the more you practice it.

Admittedly, I am still learning myself. The last progression reading I did went four cards too long. This is easy to do, because while doing a progression you are actually communing with the Divine, and that is frankly a good headspace to be in. It feels good to be in the presence of the Divine that way. So, naturally, it's easy to go too long. That talent is knowing when to stop.

In my case, there was no major damage done. I just looked at the cards, and I saw where they should have stopped, and I removed the extra cards I had laid.

Since I was writing this reading and posting it online, the querent never knew about the extra cards, and they didn't need to. If one does a reading in person, then they must be keenly aware of when to halt both the individual shuffles and the reading itself. The saying, "Practice makes perfect," absolutely applies to progression spreads when learning the shuffle stops and reading stops.

Conclusion:

So now you know three different spreads: the Celtic Cross, the three-card spread, and the progression. The Celtic Cross is not a sorcery spread; it is for entertainment. The actual spreads of the ritual are either the three-card spread or the progression. Use these, and perform the ritual correctly, and you will be well on your way to having extraordinarily accurate results.

All we have to discuss now is the required equipment.

6

Essential Equipment

When it comes to the tarot ritual, it's not that you must have specific pieces of equipment. What matters is that you have the *elements* of those specific pieces. You want to have the real stuff, yes, but it's the *intended purpose* of each piece of equipment that needs to be adhered to, not so much the exact item.

So we will look at the classic equipment, but we will also look at ways you can substitute it when you don't have the "real stuff" available. And you will find that even if you have the real stuff all set up in a special place, as I do, you will still have to substitute it quite often, because a friend will want a reading at their house, or maybe at work, or in the pub, or who knows where, and if you have your cards, you can still do the ritual.

What matters is that you know the function of the equipment so you can incorporate whatever you do have around you as a substitute. A sorcerer is clever that way; they can improvise. It's part of the wisdom of sorcery in all its forms to be able to skillfully improvise.

Having said that, we will talk about the actual equipment used in the sorcery of tarot, and we will consider how that equipment should be cared for. Caring for the equipment is actually part of the ritual itself. In fact, how we care for the equipment has a direct impact on how accurate our readings will be. So, let's examine each element in turn.

The Tarot Deck

We talked about what kind of tarot deck(s) you should own in Chapter Three. But now, assuming you have that tarot deck in your possession, how should you care for it?

The Internment Receptacle

You must inter your deck anytime you are not using it. It must be protected from outside influences. If someone picks up your deck, it affects your connection with it.

Remember, The Divine manipulates your mind; your mind in turn manipulates your brain, and your brain in turn manipulates your hands as you shuffle the deck, and the deck retains your psychic imprint from reading to reading. Thus, through continued use, it increasingly responds to your manipulation of it while you are shuffling.

After you purchase a new deck, you must be the only one who touches it. If it gets psychically contaminated by someone else using it, toss it out (or use it for scrap, or training, etc.), and get a new deck. They're not that expensive.

That said, the more expensive your deck is, the more you might want to guard it. Imagine an incredibly rare, one of a kind, deck of tarot cards; imagine you are the only sorcerer to have ever touched it since it was made. You would practically have to keep it hidden and only use it in secret, lest someone should touch it and contaminate it.

Internment is best accomplished through binding your deck with a string or ribbon and placing it in a box with a lid. Not only does this discourage other people from touching it, but it also keeps it protected from light.

Physical light is a big issue in all areas of sorcery and psychism (We will talk more about it in Chapter Seven.). Know for now that light is especially corrosive in tarot divination. If your deck stays out in the light when it's not being used, stray energies from the astral realm may contaminate it. It can build up a kind of psychic corrosion, like rust on a metal tool that's left out in the rain. So, when you're not using your deck, inter it.

Substitution Tip:

If you can't do that. If you're traveling, or if your using it away from home, and can't inter your deck, at least keep the cards in the box they originally came in.

Internment Box

Cards tied with a ribbon

The Altar

In the sorcery of ritual tarot, you perform your readings on an altar. When one thinks of an altar, an elaborate marble edifice may come to mind, but in common practice, an alter is any flat surface the cards can be shuffled on and dealt onto. Of course it could be a marble altar, but it doesn't have to be. the purpose is to have a steady, solid surface so the cards don't slide around or get dropped off the edge.

Also, the altar surface should be dark. If you're using a table, cover it with a black tablecloth. This is the best set up, but if it can't be accomplished, the flat sturdiness of the altar surface is more important than the darkness of it.

But a dark surface is the optimal surface. Again, it lessens the physical light surrounding the cards.

This is a 4-foot folding table . A black bedsheet has been draped over it and stapled to the top along the edges so as to give it a taught surface.

It's a good idea not to use your altar table for any other purpose. You shouldn't store things on top of it not related to tarot reading, and you shouldn't treat it as a temporary surface. Try to set it aside in it's own space and let that space be used for your tarot readings. This prevents stray spiritual energies from contaminating your readings when you use it. Of course, this is a somewhat minor point and may not always be possible to achieve, but it's a suggestion for better readings, nonetheless.

Candles

The less light you can use to do a tarot reading, the better. The darker it is the better. That's why candles, rather than room lights, are often used for illumination. The candles should be black if possible. Black candles are the staple for magical ceremonies, and a proper tarot reading is a magic ritual.

Black candles in glass holders

So, what if you don't have a dark place? What if your reading cards in your friends kitchen in the daylight hours? Well, there's nothing to be done about that. If you can't lower the lights and operate by candlelight, then you simply make the best of it. Pull down the blinds or shut the curtains. Turn off unnecessary lights. All of this helps.

The ideal situation is a dark room with a flat, solid table covered with a black tablecloth, using candlelight from one or two black candles. But whatever your circumstances, just try to get as close to that environment as you can. Since you understand the principles behind it, you can invent whatever you need to try to maximize some benefit by getting close to it.

Incense

The purpose of incense in any magic ritual is to attract spirit guides. This is called conjuring. In sorcery, in the past, these spirit guides were often demons that the sorcerer controlled.

Don't let this shock you, even Jesus controlled demons, and a cursory reading of the Gospel suggests that his disciples did so as well, and moreover, they were expected to.

There are demons that you can control, yourself. They are not malevolent, and your relationship of faith with the Divine makes you not only protected from any harm, but also in a position of great authority. These demons can be summoned to whisper in your mind's ear what the meaning of the cards are.

You don't have to have demons aid you, of course, and you might ask why you can't use angels instead. The fact is you can. It's really a matter of semantics. One person's angel is another person's demon, depending on their religious outlook on things. In sorcery, the term for the spiritual entity that assists you with wisdom and understanding is a demon.

A neutral term for demons or angels is *spirit guide*. And you see it used a great deal more these days. We will discuss this more in the chapter on the philosophy of darkness, but make no mistake about it, the ability to control spiritual forces, be they light or dark, the ability to use them without being affected by them is what being a sorcerer is all about.

At any rate, that's what burning incense is for, and the incense should be whatever scent you prefer. Traditionally frankincense is used for conjuring, and it's good to keep a bottle on hand, but it stinks, frankly, and while it may be the best, a nice pine or flowery scent is certainly better than nothing at all.

The incense can be burned in whatever manner you choose. Whatever you find inspiring. some sorcerers like

---

Clarification:

Demon is a modern, but inaccurate spelling of the spiritual entity under discussion. The actual spelling would be *daemon*. The difference is subtle, but a demon is usually a negative spirit, whereas in ancient lore, a daemon was a helper-demon. Gargoyles on old buildings are an example of a sculpture of a daemon. Tarot demons would actually be daemons.

to use self-igniting charcoal in an iron cauldron and sprinkle the incense on that. Some use a stick of incense in a holder, and some use a small cone of incense in a holder of some sort. It's really whatever you feel is more effective from your psychic perspective.

Stick incense in a holder; a bottle of frankincense, and a small iron cauldron for burning incense. All readily available at Amazon.com

---

Substitution Tip:

So, what if you don't have incense? Keep in mind, it's only one element of the ritual. If you have it, you'll be more accurate in your interpretations. If you don't, you may still be more than sufficiently accurate for any general reading. You can always substitute it with flowers, a spritz of perfume in the air, or even smoke, if you like the smell of some kind of smoke. Use your imagination.

Music

Music has two effects in a tarot ritual: If it's played softly in the background, it can be relaxing and thus put your mind at ease and allow for greater psychic intuition when your interpreting the cards.

The second effect, again, is to attract spirits to aid you in the magic ritual. You see this in other religions as well. Buddhist use a gong in their temples; Catholics ring bells during the consecration of the host, Muslims sing prayers out over loudspeakers five times a day. And most churches sing hymns or have bands.

For your tarot rituals, you can simply play some soft music in the background.

The best kind of music is instrumental music. Music with lyrics can be very distracting and can insert thoughts into your head while you're trying to understand the meaning of the cards.

If you don't have any music, again, it's just one element of the ritual. You'll be more accurate with it, but you may be accurate enough without it.

Substitution Tip:

So, what if you don't have any music? In that case, try to find a quiet place. Nothing is worse than noisy distractions. The best music, if you don't have anything else is silence.

Conclusion

So, above is the essential equipment for the sorcery of ritual tarot. Taken together, they can seriously enhance the accuracy of your readings. If you use the equipment in its best forms, and if you care for your cards, you will see much greater validation in your readings, and it will amaze you.

The good news is, none of this equipment is expensive. You can find most, if not all, of it at Walmart, certainly at Amazon.com.

How elaborate you get with it, of course, is up to you, your level of commitment, and your financial means. You can have an entire room dedicated to it. You could have an entire temple dedicated to it if you're so inclined. Or you   could have it all in a briefcase that you can take with you to any location. Or you can have both. It's really all up to your imagination as a sorcerer of the dark art of Tarot.

7

A Philosophy of Darkness

Introduction

People have an aversion to the dark side. When they think of dark magic or dark sorcery, they think of something evil. The difference between white magic and black magic, everyone knows, for instance, is that white magic does helpful spells and black magic does harmful spells.

But when we talk about darkness, we are not talking about black magic. They are not the same thing. Sorcery is a dark art, but sorcery is not black magic.

When we talk about darkness, one should not associate it with those antisocial personality types found all over the web these days, especially in Facebook groups. We all know the type: they revel in horrible looking knives, blood and gore photos, bodies covered in horrific tattoos of skulls and hateful words. Piercings in every manner so as to make their bodies look mutilated and tortured, and of course, there is the sex. Sex in everything, and it's always seems to be displayed as nothing less than sadistic bondage. That sort of thing is black—but that is not darkness.

Darkness is not about animal cruelty or sacrificing children. It is not about committing crimes or placing curses on coworkers, and it has nothing to do with devil worship or selling one's soul to Satan. Again, those things are *black*, but that's not what darkness is. That's not even what darkness means.

Darkness is not immoral; it is not sin. Darkness is not hateful and cruel, and darkness is not antichrist or demonic. Rather, darkness is the goal of all spiritual development.

Everyone is looking for darkness whether they know it or not. It is a primal drive in the psyche of humankind. Everyone is looking for darkness, because we are spiritually designed to escape the light.

The Nature of Light

When we talk about darkness, we mean precisely what it means—no light. And this is not symbolic. Darkness means no light, *no physical light*, no photons. It rests on the principle that light is the curtain between the astral plane and the physical world.

Photons of light, in one form or another, make up the entire physical world. The photons of light extend through the entire electromagnetic spectrum. So, light is not just the white light you see in the daytime or when you flick on a switch. Light actually is a broad spectrum of energy that is the ultimate substance of all matter in the universe. This is a scientific fact.

THE ELECTROMAGNETIC SPECTRUM

Wavelength (meters)

Radio	Microwave	Infrared	Visible	Ultraviolet	X-Ray	Gamma Ray
10^{-3}	10^{-2}	10^{-5}	10^{-6}	10^{-8}	10^{-10}	10^{-12}

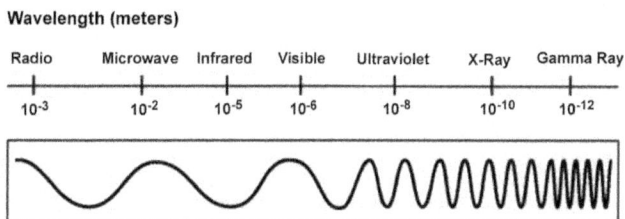

Quantum mechanics is also a scientific fact, and it shows us that light is a very strange thing. It seems to be both physical and non-physical at the same time. It actually changes from a wave to a particle when it is observed by a conscious mind. There is no explanation for this. It is one of the strangest realities of nature.

But light behaves like this because it is the membrane separating the physical from the astral. It is on the cusp of both, and so it behaves like both.

Just beyond light is the astral plane. If you were able to part light like a curtain, you would be looking at the astral plane. But light blinds us—it shields our minds from perceiving the astral plane.

That blinding is what we call *incarnation*. It means that your mind is in the physical world; literally, your mind is interned in a physical body.

But make no mistake, you are still on the astral plane. You are still residing in your astral kingdom, but you are staring at the light and your mind has gone past that light into the physical world, and there's no getting back until your body dies. When we die, and no longer perceive light in any capacity, we instantly find ourselves sitting on the astral plane. Take away light, and you have the astral plane. It's that simple.

Right now, at this very moment, even as you are reading these words, you are in your astral kingdom just sitting there staring into the light. It is a light source the Divine brought to you when it was decided that you would incarnate. It's like a box, and he handed it to you, and you opened it; and when you did, you saw the light therein, and you couldn't look away, and you fell into it and through it—mentally speaking—until you were on the other side of it.

Right now, you are not moving; you are not blinking; you are just staring, and what you are seeing, as you stare into the light, is your life here in the physical world.

The light is so blinding, in fact, and you've been staring at it for so long, that you believe the life you are looking at is real, but it is not real; it's illusory, and the light makes that illusion look real. But the true reality of things is the astral plane—pure and simple. Quite literally, we are blinded by the light. The light—physical light—is playing a trick on us.

The Astral Plane

The astral plane is always there, and you are always on the astral plane at all times. You never leave it. What you are doing on the astral plane right at this moment is staring into the aforementioned light.

The astral plane is your home—it is home in the truest sense of the word. It's where you were created; it's where your core personality eternally exists. Just as a dream character lives in the dream world that your mind creates, so you exist as a creation of the Divine Mind on the astral plane.

A deep person, an old soul, an evolved human mind, wants to go home. It doesn't want to stay here in the fakeness of the physical world. So, it is attracted to darkness—because it wants to escape the light.

Don't get me wrong: I'm not suggesting that when darkness and light are used as metaphors for ignorance or wisdom respectively that an old soul wants to be ignorant. No. When we talk about light and dark, we are talking literally about the physical world (which is entirely made of light) and the astral plane (which is entirely void of light).

The place where you really exist, has no light, no light of any kind. That doesn't mean you can't see. What it means is that on the astral plane you don't use light in order to see.

So, that's why there's a fascination with the dark. Serious spirituality is almost always clothed in darkness—literally. Priests and nuns wear dark. Greek Orthodox priests wear dark; dark is worn at funerals; witches wear dark, and goths are all about darkness. Dark is attractive to wear, because dark symbolizes spiritual depth. We even close our eyes when we pray.

The spiritual need to escape light is also apparent in our tarot ritual. We do everything we can to have as little as possible. We shut off the lights and light black candles. We cover our table with a black cloth. We keep our cards in a dark box. We do whatever we can to get less light, so we are more aware of things astrally. This is the fundamental philosophy of darkness.

Darkness is not about sin or taboo. It's about getting rid of the light so we can see the astral plane. When we say then that tarot is a *dark* art, we are saying that it is used to connect with the astral plane. We use the cards to get back passed the curtain of light to gain wisdom from the beings on our astral plane, beings such as our spirit guides.

Why is darkness associated with evil?

So, why then is darkness so often associated with evil? The simple answer is fear. People are so hopelessly deluded by the appearance of physical life that they believe it is all that exists. They believe that when they are dead, they cease to be—just as if they never had been created in the first place.

When you show these people the curtain of light, and you suggest they step beyond it to the astral plane, all they can think of is ceasing to exist, all they can think of is everything they have to lose. Thus they associate death with depression, loss, and grief.

The truth is that nothing we have in this so-called life is any more real than the objects you had in last night's dream. When you die, the light will go out, and you will be able to see your astral kingdom again—and most people are vastly more wealthy in the astral realm than they are in the illusion of a life here in the physical world.

But then again, some are not. Some have barren, desolate astral kingdoms. Lonely places that produce no wealth at all. Their astral existence is what we would call hell. What Jesus would have called *the place of weeping and gnashing of teeth*. The whole reason God incarnated these tragic minds was to get them out of that astral suffering. God was being merciful to them.

However, if they don't do anything in this life to fix things in their astral kingdom, then dying physically means only a return to hell, and somewhere down deep they know it. They sense it *psychically*. And so they fear death and darkness.

Because it is such a wide-spread notion that darkness is bad, we can assume a lot of people have very desolate kingdoms they came from and will return to.

But that's not the case with you! You have taken up the tarot cards. You have put on the mantle of the sorcerer.

You now have a new connection with the Divine and with your spirit guides. You don't have to be afraid anymore. The demons aren't dragging you into the darkness—you own the darkness, and the daemons now serve you and wait like faithful pets for the day you return to your astral kingdom. You are the sorcerer! You are a child of the Divine Creator!

And that, my friend, is the philosophy of darkness.

About the Author

Edward Gordon is an author and tarot reader and the owner of one of the largest and most popular psychic reading groups on Facebook, *Free Psychic Readings*. His previous works include, *Caretakers of Eternity*, *Vital Architecture and the New Design of Happiness*, and *The Veridican Gospel of Jesus Christ*. He is currently working on his second novel and resides in the New Orleans area of the United States.

Edward's Website:

EdwardGordonBooks.com

Edward's E-mail:

Edward@EdwardGordonBooks.com